# You Saw Me
# on the Radio

## SWAIM-PAUP SPORTS SERIES

Sponsored by James C. '74 and Debra Parchman Swaim
and T. Edgar '74 and Nancy Paup

# You Saw Me on the Radio

## Recollections and Favorite Calls as the Voice of Aggie Athletics

## Dave South

Foreword by Alan Cannon

Texas A&M University Press • College Station

Copyright © 2019 by Dave South
First edition

This paper meets the requirements of ANSI/NISO
Z39.48-1992 (Permanence of Paper).
Binding materials have been chosen for durability.
Manufactured in the United States of America
∞

Library of Congress Control Number: 2019943263

ISBN 13: 978-1-62349-809-2 (cloth: alk. paper)
ISBN 978-1-62349-810-8 (Ebook)

# Contents

# Foreword

Growing up, I was blessed to be raised in a family who had a love of sports and sports stories. Early on, my parents bought me a baseball mitt, a football, and a basketball and a hoop in the driveway. My dad would take me to the Cotton Bowl to watch the Dallas Cowboys, Moody Coliseum to watch the Dallas Chaparrals, Fair Park Coliseum to watch the Dallas Blackhawks, and Turnpike Stadium (renamed Arlington Stadium when the Washington Senators moved to Texas to become the Texas Rangers). My mom was just as supportive, as I spent many a Mother's Day at Preston Trails Country Club watching the Byron Nelson Golf Tournament.

I loved going through the box scores and reading stories in the newspaper, listening to radio broadcasts of games, and watching televised sports whenever possible. Those radio broadcasts painted a wonderful picture in my mind, and I thought the world of the broadcasters.

I have had the good fortune of being around Aggie athletics since the 1970s, first as a fan and then working in the sports information office as a student, later working on the staff in a full-time role. During this time, I have met a lot of wonderful people with great stories.

Perhaps the greatest blessing has been the opportunity to get to know a man whom I believe has seen more Aggie athletics events than any other person: Dave South. Dave is known as "The Voice of Aggieland." He handled radio play-by-play duties for Texas A&M football, basketball, and baseball from the 1980s and continues to call Aggie baseball action. Back before every game was on television, you would scan the radio dial for that familiar voice that let you know you had tuned in to an Aggie athletics event.

A Hall of Fame announcer with an unmistakable voice, Dave's knowledge of the game and his passion for the players and coaches always came through in his broadcasts. It was amazing to watch him prepare for his life's work—he knew just the right time to interject statistics into the broadcast.

Dave has taken the time to put into words in this excellent book some of his stories and experiences from calling Aggie athletics events on the radio.

Some of my own personal memories with Dave include running across the Golden Gate Bridge, helping him squeeze his football crew into small radio booths, making do with whatever makeshift baseball announcement area we found ourselves in, including the front porch at Olsen Field. There is one event that, to this day, Dave hasn't forgiven me for.

Traveling with Coach Shelby Metcalf and the Aggie basketball team back in the day required a good bit of commercial travel, and the radio guy and the sports information director traveled together on most trips. On one trip to Fayetteville, Dave and I had flown commercial. After we had been beaten and with bad weather coming in at the airport, one seat opened up with the team on one of the small university prop planes coming back to Aggieland. I turned and wished Dave all the best and looked forward to seeing him when he got back to College Station. As it turned it out, it would be a few days down the road!

I look forward to reading and reliving many of these outstanding stories from Dave about his time here in Aggieland. Over the years of working and traveling with Dave, I have come to hold him in even higher esteem—not because of his outstanding broadcasting work, but as a role model. A Christian, a husband, a father, a grandfather, and a friend, Dave has his priorities in order—faith, family, and Aggie athletics. Dave, we appreciate you taking the time to write this inspiring book, and we appreciate all you have given to Aggieland!

Alan Cannon
Associate Athletics Director / Communications
Texas A&M University

# Preface

My generation was raised on the radio. I think I was eight years old before we could afford a television set. It was a great big floor model that was loaded with electronic tubes.

When a tube went out, you could go to a convenience store with as many as two or three tubes that might be bad. You would put the male end of the tube in a female slot, and the tube tester would tell you if it was bad or good. The store kept the replacement tubes in a cabinet. In those days, we had only three television channels. Wichita Falls had two (CBS and NBC), and Lawton, Oklahoma, 50 miles to the north, had one (ABC). For good reception, you needed an outside antenna, and for a weak signal, you had rabbit ears.

Radio helped us develop an imagination. We had to conjure up in our heads what was being described on the radio. I listened to Gene Autry, Gang Busters, Tarzan, Amos and Andy, Jack Benny, Burns and Allen, Arthur Godfrey, Don McNeill's Breakfast Club, and many more. We had to use our imaginations as Gene and his sidekick Smiley Burnette were riding their horses and chasing the outlaws.

How could a good radio show affect you? Let me tell this story. When my sons, Randy and Michael, were nine and six, respectively, we went on a late-night road trip.

CBS Radio at that time ran a show at 10:00 p.m. called *The CBS Mystery Theatre*. Both boys were in the backseat, and I was alone up front in the driver's seat. I will admit that the Saturday-night edition was more frightening than the weeknight version. About 15 minutes into the program, both boys had climbed over into the front seat and were sitting as close to me as they could get. Their imaginations were running wild!

This brings me to this book's title. There was a fellow I used to listen to who had one of the best radio voices I think I ever heard. I had never met him, but his voice projected, and I had an image in my mind of what he looked like. I imagined him standing about 6′4″ or 6′5″ and weighing at least 250 pounds. And he would have a firm, strong handshake. Our first time meeting in person was not at all what I expected. This big "booming voice" belonged to a man less than 5′10″ tall and weighing in at about 160. He did, however, have a firm handshake.

So what did my voice project to Aggie fans who had never met me? I found out from one lady whom I met in San Antonio and Aggie Park. Here's the conversation:

FAN: Someone said you are Dave South.
ME: Yes, ma'am, I am.
FAN: No, you're not.
ME: Yes, I'm Dave South.
FAN: I don't believe you.
ME: Why not?
FAN: I had this picture of you in my head that you were short, fat, and bald-headed.

I have no idea who the woman was, but I do thank her for the idea for this book title.

# You Saw Me
# on the Radio

# ① How It All Got Started

## In the Beginning

If you've ever played golf, there are those moments when you hit the ball and someone behind you says, "I'm sorry, I was talking in your backswing." My reply has always been the same, "That's OK, I talk for a living."

That is exactly what I've have been doing since the 1960s, starting with DJ work (along with sports and news) at three radio stations in Wichita Falls and then moving into collegiate sports broadcasting in 1970.

My interest in sports play-by-play started at the age of 10 because of baseball. I joined my first little league team in the spring of 1952, when the coach asked me to put on oversized catching gear and move behind the plate. I was six years old and wouldn't turn seven until August. I knew nothing about the rules and not a whole lot about the various positions on the field, but it was love at first play for me and the game of baseball.

My parents bought me a three-fingered Stan Musial glove (about seven dollars, as I recall) and a cheap baseball at Sears. The bat would come much later, as they were more expensive. With my glove and ball, I would go behind Lamar Baptist Church and play catch off the wall. Occasionally, I could find a friend for a game of catch.

In 1955, I discovered live coverage of major league baseball on the radio. It was the Mutual Game of the Day, which consisted mostly of Chicago Cub games, since at that time, they played only day games.

I started collecting bubble gum baseball cards that same year. The cards that seemed come up most often for me were those featuring the Brooklyn Dodgers.

I found out from my father that at night after the sun went down, you could listen to the Saint Louis Cardinals on KMOX out of St. Louis, which was his team. He wanted me to pull for the Cards, but it was too late, I had fallen in love with the Dodgers.

I noticed that my little league coach had a scorebook where he would write down the lineup and keep track of the game. I remember asking him if I could look at it and asking him to explain it to me. He did and even tore out a page and gave it to me.

When I got home that night, I got a pencil, paper, and ruler and made my own scoresheets—actually, I made dozens of them. With my own scoresheets, I would listen to a Mutual game, score it, and then go to my bedroom, raise up the window, and recreate that game looking out on my backyard. I had an audience of one, my dog, Rin Tin Tin. That was the beginning of my career in sports play-by-play.

I still have all my baseball cards. My Stan Musial glove only lasted a year because I played all the time. I did get a bat during the 1955 season and named it the Dodger Slugger. I wished I had saved those scoresheets with my make-believe games.

In 1957, at the age of 12, I took a major step forward and went to work at a radio station. It was located in the closet of my bedroom on McNeil Street in Wichita Falls, Texas. The inspiration came from my family's weekly shopping trips on Thursdays.

In the 1950s in Wichita Falls, stores stayed open late only one night a week. Thursday night you could shop as late as 9 o'clock. My dad was off Thursday afternoons from the A&P food store on 9th Street. Mother would pack a meal for the four of us (sister Judy was there), and we would head downtown. This was not a favorite time for me because I was bored to tears.

One of the radio stations, KSYD 990 on the dial, had a studio window on the street in downtown Wichita Falls. I discovered this on one of our early trips. I stood at the window looking at the DJ, watching everything he did. There was a speaker above that window, so I could hear everything he said. Every Thursday night I was there, and he would wave to me and sometimes say something about me on the radio.

Weeks went by, and then one night in December it was cold, and he invited me to sit in the control room and watch the action up close. I asked him all kinds of questions, and he answered them all. He even gave me old UPI wire copy and commercial radio scripts to take home.

One of the best jobs for a boy of 12 in those days was throwing the newspaper. I had a route that I took both morning and afternoon. The paper was the *Wichita Falls Times and Record News*. My route was big enough that I made pretty good money.

I was responsible for paying for my school clothes, school lunches, haircuts, and anything extra from the grocery store. What I had left over, I started to save. With those savings, I purchased the equipment I would need to start my closet radio station. There were two 45 rpm record players, a sound mixer, two tape recorders, a microphone, a headset, a card table, and a stool.

I don't remember when I went on the air in that closet studio, but I do remember that my call letters were KDAV. I spent hours each week in my closet studio recording on a reel-to-reel tape recorder each hour of what I thought to be four-star radio.

I didn't take a lunch break, though my mother would bring me a sandwich, cookies, and a glass of milk. After all, I had an audience to entertain! Neighborhood boys would come over and join me as guests on the show. Mother started listening to some of my recordings and would correct my grammar or suggest phrases to use.

Like the old scoresheets, none of the tapes survived. KDAV would stay on the air in my closet until I was about 16. The broadcasts were interrupted only by school, baseball, church, and the occasional family vacation.

KDAV went off the air when I landed my first job at a real radio station. It was the early days of FM radio, and we had an FM station in Wichita Falls. When I applied for the job, they asked me to record an audition tape. I read some news stories and a piece of commercial copy.

I was in high school by this time and took every speech course that was offered. I was fortunate to learn from who I believed was one of the best speech teachers around, Dr. Bedford Furr.

When I finished the audition tape, the program director, Mike Hoy, started listening to it. He suddenly stopped the tape and looked at me and asked, "Where have you worked before?" I told him I listened to the radio all the time and learned from the people on the air. I couldn't bring myself to tell him about KDAV and my closet broadcast career.

Not many people had FM radios in those days. They were expensive, and they certainly were not in cars. I still believe that when I was on the air at the FM station, I didn't have many more listeners than I did when recreating those baseball games from my bedroom window for my dog Rin Tin Tin. . . . but I was working in radio.

I would work in radio all through school before moving to Austin to work for a television station. In 1967, I was laid off and called a radio station in Waco about a possible job opening. General manager Frank Fallon interviewed me over the phone and offered me the position. Meeting Frank opened doors for me into sports broadcasting at the college and at the professional level, including the newly formed Southwest Conference Radio Network.

## How I Got Started at Texas A&M

When I worked for the Exxon Network, and then the Southwest Conference Radio Network, the announcers would float around and not be assigned to a specific school. At the end of the 1984 season, I told network officials that I was not going to return the next year. I had started with the Exxon Network in 1970 and the SWC in 1974, for a combined total of 14 seasons.

My sales position at a radio station in Waco had really taken off, and I felt I needed to focus on that job. Back then, you couldn't make a living on the salary from a radio play-by-play job—it was the side job you took to supplement your full-time job. My sales position was my primary job, and I just felt like I needed to pay attention to what I was doing.

That spring of 1985, I got a call from the late Ralph Carpenter, who was the sports information director at Texas A&M. He said, "I've heard that you're not coming back next year, that you're going to quit." I said yes, and Ralph told me that the guy they had lined up to do the games for the 1985 season had elected to go back to his home school in Missouri, which was Southwest Missouri State as I recall. He asked if I'd be willing to broadcast the Texas A&M games for one year while they looked for somebody.

I talked about it to my wife, Leanne. Her dad had gone to A&M, and I had a deep respect for the university. I really did. My sixth-grade teacher was Mary Todd, and her husband was Dick Todd. Dick was an All-American at Texas A&M and the head football coach at Midwestern University in Wichita Falls. Occasionally, he would come up to the school and play football with the boys on the playground and talk about Texas A&M!

Leanne and I decided that I'd go down and work the football games for Texas A&M for one year. I went down and met with Coach Sherrill, and we seemed to hit it off. For the next three years, I thought we worked well together.

So I started doing Texas A&M games with the idea that this would last for one year. When I stepped away from Aggie football after the 2017 season, that one year had turned into 32, and my broadcasting responsibilities expanded to include men's basketball and baseball.

It's been a blessing to have broadcast these games, especially for that length of time. That doesn't happen a whole lot these days, but it did happen for me. And for as long as I have been in sports broadcasting, my play-by-play job was never my primary source of income. It supplemented my family's income and led to some incredible experiences and memories.

## ② Behind the Scenes

As I have reflected on my 47-year career in radio and as a sports broadcaster, I think it is fair to say that technology revolutionized how we did our jobs—and yet the process for broadcasting a game stayed rather consistent. It is crystal clear to me that my success can be attributed, in part, to the wonderful people with whom I was fortunate enough to work. I hope the stories that follow give you a sense of the "nuts and bolts" of how we broadcast a game on the radio and tell you who just a few of the unsung folks were who helped us broadcast Texas Aggie football.

### Broadcast Technology: What a Change!

Over my 45-plus years in radio, I would say changes in technology played a major role in how the work of broadcasters changed over time.

### Broadcast Loop: One-Way Telephone Transmission

Today, the games on radio are almost all broadcast over the internet. In 1970, they were done over a broadcast loop. This was a one-way, more sophisticated telephone line provided by the phone company, and it was expensive. If a game was played on the West Coast, the cost to broadcast the game from that location would easily run more than $900.

Not only would you have to install the broadcast loop, but you also needed a normal telephone line so you could communicate with the studio back in Texas. Sometimes, to keep the expenses down, the network would delete the normal telephone line.

Jim Hawthorne, the former Louisiana State University (LSU) broadcaster, told a story about a high-school game he was covering. They had a broadcast loop but no telephone line, and there was no phone in the press box. He set up the equipment and fed crowd noise down the line so he could walk one block to a pay phone to make sure the station could hear the noise being sent. This was long before cell phones.

Jim then went back to the booth, and he and his partner broadcast the game. After the game, he went back to the pay phone, only to find out that before the game started, the station had lost the line. That night, only he and the color analyst heard the game.

There were times when your line would cross paths with another line. In those instances, the broadcast team wouldn't know it because the broadcast loop was a one-way communication. However, the normal phone line you were crossed up with could hear the game. This happened to me once. I was working a basketball game when the game's broadcast popped up in the middle of a telephone conversation between two older ladies. They were on the air with the game, laughing and carrying on, wondering if the radio audience could hear them. The answer was yes—they were on the radio!

## ISDN: Entering the Digital Age

Later, the broadcast loop gave way to an integrated services digital network, or ISDN line. Still sent over telephone lines, the digital signal delivered a better sound to listeners. By that time, cell phones had become popular and served as the backup if any problems arose with the ISDN line.

There were two instances, against Texas Tech in Lubbock and against Sam Houston State in Huntsville, where we had to broadcast an Aggie basketball game using a cell phone.

After the Sam Houston game, Coach Melvin Watkins's wife, Burrell, asked why we didn't broadcast the game. I said we did. Burrell said she had sat right across from us, and all we did was talk on the phone!

## MP3s and Stats on Steroids

Up until the last dozen years or more, most of the games dating back to the 1970s were not recorded. All those broadcasts are lost forever. MP3 recording changed all that. Not only did the network record the games, but I did too. Starting in 2006, I recorded all of my broadcasts for football, basketball, and baseball.

I have mentioned statistics programs in one of the stories in this book. One stat program, Stat Broadcast, works for all three sports and gives you so much information that you can't use it all. In football, for example, you can touch a player's name on the screen, and if he is a receiver, you can look at each catch he made that day.

Stat programs, instant access to the teams' game notes and stats on the internet, MP3 recordings, and the convenience of online editing programs has made life easier for all of us. Young broadcasters today have no idea about the challenges broadcasters faced in the '70s, just like I have no idea what a broadcaster's life was like in the '40s and '50s.

## Getting Ready

What I will explain here was typical for me, and likely a lot of other play-by-play announcers, when getting ready for a game.

Start-up (before the first game) took the most time, since we were building not only the other team's spotter board (explained in this book) but also the board for Texas A&M. We had to wait until both coaches announced a two-deep, which had to be typed into place with name, hometown, height, weight, and classification. This would occur a week to 10 days out from the first kick-off.

For the Aggies, I would meet with the OC and DC and get the top 30 players on both sides of the ball. That number would more than cover the two-deep and give me at least eight more players who were likely to play.

Did that always work? No, it did not. There would always be three or four more who would be added as we got closer to the season and even after the first couple of games.

Getting the other team's two-deep always presented a challenge. There were times when the opponent's coach did not want to release his depth chart before the first game. You would get the starters and the SID's best guess as to who would be the backups.

During the two years the Aggies played UCLA in back-to-back seasons, there was no two-deep given, and I am not sure who made that decision.

There was one season, during the first game, where the coach just said to give them the entire roster: "I have no idea who is going to play or not play." What was sad about that circumstance was that it was a coach I had worked with, and I considered him to be a friend. Believe me, he knew, but what made me feel a little better about it was that his announcer wasn't given a two-deep either. That coach, by the way, was on the hot seat going into that year, which may have been a reason we didn't get a two-deep.

Once the season started, the stats after the first game would show the participation chart, who ran the ball, who caught the ball, which QBs took part, who made tackles for the defense, and who returned punts and kick-offs. So game two was more complete, and we felt like the spotter boards would do what they were supposed to do.

Before every game, we looked at all the stats (including opponents') to see if someone suddenly appeared on one side of the ball or the other, and then we would add them to the board. The internet made life much easier for all of us: the complete stat package would be available almost as soon as the previous game was over.

We also had a final book, which had everything we needed on the last game, and as the season moved on, we had a book on every game that had been played (this meant lots of reading).

I liked to look at the last two books and go over every play from both of those games. I did the same thing for Texas A&M.

That book had a running account of each play: down, distance, yard line, and time in the game. That made it easy to review what a team did on each down, especially third downs. This information was good to use on the radio show the following week.

As the season neared, I would load the recordings of the last three or four games A&M had played the year before on my iPod, and when I was working in the office or working out at the gym, I would listen to each game.

That practice never stopped once MP3 recordings were made available as the equipment changed, as you could easily record every game right there in the radio booth. If we were playing a team that the Aggies had played the year before, I would go back and listen to that game to refresh my memory.

Sunday afternoon in my home office, the work began on the next game. If A&M had played the day before, I listened from beginning to end to all that was said on the radio the previous day. I always made it a habit to listen with a critical ear. I hoped that approach would make me a little bit better before the next broadcast.

I have donated every recording of every game that was taped going back to 2007 to the A&M Archives. Prior to MP3, the games were put on cassette, but that technology would not last, so all of those games are lost forever.

Each school prepared a press release with notes and facts about the team, coaches, players, current stats, and career stats. Those were normally ready by Monday at noon, and I would get a highlighter and start looking for anything that would be of interest to the fan listening to the radio.

I spent Tuesday night filling out the A&M board (stats on the players) and Wednesday night working on the opponent board. The opponent spotter board was completed on Sunday afternoon, so it would be ready when I did my Wednesday prep. Thursday and Friday was memory work. I had to memorize every Aggie player and his number before the season started. The opponent top 30 on each side of the ball had to be done on Thursday and Friday.

Something that I did going back to 1985 was save every final stat book from each game the Aggies played—not only in football but also in basketball and baseball. That was invaluable in doing research to prepare for a team that we had played before, especially conference games.

When the 2017 football season ended and the 2017–2018 basketball season was complete, I took all those files, like I did with the game recordings, and donated them to the Texas A&M Archives. These files could be valuable for future research.

I enjoyed the games, and I enjoyed them more when the Aggies would win. However, for those of us who worked the games, it was just that—work.

Tailgating never happened for any of us. By the time that we (sports news writers, broadcasters, etc.) got out of the stadium, everyone was gone, and we found a deserted parking lot. Then on Sunday, for those same people, the work started on the next game.

I've told some of my close friends that the fall of 2018 would be the first that I have not worked seven days a week in a very long time.

## The Working Radio Booth

There are several photos in this book from different broadcasts recognizing those who helped in the radio booth. For Texas A&M football radio broadcasts, the crew consisted of the engineer, the play-by-play announcer, the color analyst, the sideline reporter, offensive and defensive spotters, the yardage-wheel person, and the reader-card handler.

We've gotten questions through the years asking who was on our broadcast team and what happened "behind the scenes" in the radio booth during a Texas A&M football game. We even selected several photos from different broadcasts where we recognized those who helped in the radio booth.

I am choosing football because basketball and baseball were much simpler to broadcast, and the broadcast space was usually near the fans, so people attending the games could see the radio broadcaster in action.

So here's my answer to what happened in the broadcast booth before, during, and after an Aggie football game.

The engineer arrived in the booth first, some four hours before kickoff (I have more to say about the three men who engineered during my tenure later in this section). On the road, he pulled a large, heavy equipment case that contained everything needed to air the game. The engineers during my tenure at Texas A&M were Ed Hadden, Andrew Hicks, and Randy South.

The first task was to check the internet lines to make sure they were in working order. If they weren't, the engineer would contact that school's IT staff to correct the problem. Next, he set up the mixer (control board) and plugged in the headsets, cables, and power cords.

Once the equipment was set up, he called the studios in Jefferson City, Missouri, and the board operator (also called the board op) who would work the game that day. They sound-checked each of the mics and the sound level on the sideline reporter's mic.

Stadiums on game day needed an amazing number of two-way radio frequencies. Just imagine all the different groups that used frequencies during a game—radio, television, security, each football team, public address, EMTs, concessions, sound technicians, and home-team event management, just to name a few.

For the Aggie broadcast, the engineer contacted that stadium's sound techs for the radio frequency assigned to our sideline reporter. Once the mics were checked out and working, someone would make their way to the A&M locker room to set up the communications for the postgame show.

Often the location was not a conducive place for the coach to talk. Phone lines had to be strung along the walls to a more suitable spot. That equipment also had to be picked up after the game. This work had to be done by two people: one to talk from the radio booth and one who was located in the locker room.

That equipment would be turned off and then turned on again at the conclusion of the game. You may remember the 2012 Alabama game. Before the game, the line was checked out, and it sounded great. When it was turned on after the game, it was stone-cold dead. During the biggest game of the year and of Kevin Sumlin's career at Texas A&M, we had no postgame with the head coach.

After the engineer finished the setup, I moved to my spot in the booth. The radio booth at almost every location had a lower position and an upper position. The play-by-play man and color analyst were in the lower position. A good example of this is the cover shot for this book. That shot also shows my spotter boards and a computer.

I liked to work with an offensive board and a defensive board. One side had the A&M offense, and the reverse side had our opponents. The same thing was true for the defensive board.

These were metal boards that would work with magnets. We would line up names of the players in offensive and defensive formations and list players' names, numbers, weights, heights, hometowns, classifications, and current stats.

I used a defensive spotter and an offensive spotter. Each of these fellows would place a magnet next to the 22 players who were out on the field. When a player made a catch, a run, or a big defensive play, a red magnet would be placed by his number.

When working as a spotter, you could not act like a fan—you had to stay focused on what was happening down on the field.

Mike Lednecky and Byran Farris were my spotters for several years. Mike worked offense, and Byran worked defense. It helped that they were former students and loved Aggie football.

At Kyle Field, Dave Elmendorf sat to my right and would come in at the conclusion of a play and comment on or describe what happened.

Will Johnson was our sideline reporter and reported on injuries, interviewed the coach at halftime, described field conditions, and delivered weather updates—in other words, anything he felt added to the broadcast. I hired Will as a student worker and am proud of what he has done with his career at Texas A&M.

Bob Davis was another member of our team. Bob had a round disk that we called the yardage wheel. He wore a mic during the game, but only Dave Elmendorf and I could hear him. If a play went for more than 10 yards, he gave us the yards gained on the play as well as the yardage on punts and punt returns.

The last member of the team was Bill Cross, who handled the reader cards that we used to promote sponsors and sponsored segments.

There could be as many as 60 to 70 of these cards. Every one of them had to be read to fulfill sponsorship contracts. Bill would always have a card ready anytime the game allowed for a read.

Our radio booth and setup would be like any other one would find at either a college game or a professional game.

Spotter boards varied from broadcaster to broadcaster, and mine changed almost every year if I thought a new design would work better. The board featured in this book was the last one I used for the A&M offense, when the Aggies played in the Belk Bowl.

The crew we used worked well together and loved Aggie football. It was a happy booth when Texas A&M was winning and not so happy when the Aggies weren't. We shared some very good times together, and we will always be friends.

Just about any broadcaster would ask for the windows to be opened so they could hear the crowd. All announcers fed off the excitement of the crowd, even on the road.

When the windows couldn't be opened, there was a small window at the top of the wall near the ceiling that would open so the engineer could drop a mic out to get the crowd noise, but it was not the same.

Normally our booth would be near the 40- or 45-yard line, but not always. The broadcast booth at AT&T Stadium in Arlington was in the end zone and at such an angle that we were looking up the field to call the game. Depth perception from that location was difficult at best. We ended up calling some plays at the far end by looking at the video board.

Other unexpected problems would pop up from time to time. One such time was in Hattiesburg, Mississippi, when Texas A&M was playing Southern Mississippi. It was a very hot, humid day, and as the game got into the second quarter, moisture started to cover the window (yes, it was a closed booth). We literally could not see the field.

I had just commented that we needed to go outside and squeegee the window. Southern Mississippi had experienced this problem before and was ready. Out of nowhere came a student with a squeegee on a 10-foot pole. He spent the rest of the game going from one end of the press box to the other keeping the windows clear. It felt like we were sitting in a full-service gas station!

Normally the connections and power supply the engineer needed when setting up the booth were on the second level where he usually sat.

But in one radio booth, everything was down where Dave and I were working. Every wire had to be run over some pipes along the ceiling and then connected below the table where our material sat.

When this was all connected, I commented during the broadcast that it looked like a Radio Shack had exploded in the booth. There were wires everywhere.

In another booth, there was a support column that held the ceiling up. This column was right in the middle of the table the engineer used. He had to sit on one side of the column with the mixer while everything else (equipment-wise) was on the other side of the column.

Earlier I mentioned the engineers who worked the broadcast with me at Texas A&M. These three men were all good at what they did and kept us on the air. A crucial part of their job was repacking the equipment after road games.

They were under pressure to pack up and get the trunk down to the Aggie football equipment truck and then hustle to get on the bus to the airport. We never wanted the team buses to wait on the radio crew, and they never had to thanks to these three fellows.

## The Pregame Show

This is a look at what happens between the studio board operator and the radio crew at the game site leading up to the radio broadcast of a game.

The broadcast starts with a recorded opening that leads into the pregame show. I'm using a basketball broadcast as the example. What I'm describing here is the same for football and baseball. The only difference is the length of the pregame shows. Football's pregame starts one hour before kickoff. Basketball's pregame is 30 minutes long, and baseball's pregame only lasts 15 minutes before first pitch.

At the game site, we set up the radio equipment and establish an internet connection back to the studio. From the studio, the game is sent to the radio stations that carry Texas A&M games.

Throughout the years, these studios have been in Dallas and Oklahoma City and are now in Jefferson City, Missouri. In all three locations, there is a person called the board operator, or board op, responsible for counting down when a broadcast is to begin as well as when the broadcast is coming out of a commercial break. This countdown is used by the stations carrying the game and the announcers at the game site.

The countdown for basketball normally starts 30 minutes before the game. It goes something like this: If the game starts at 7:00 p.m., the pregame starts at 6:30 p.m. At 6:00 p.m., the network starts playing instrumental music. At 6:15 p.m., a recorded voice says, "Tonight's broadcast will begin fifteen minutes from my mark. . . . Five, four, three, two, one, mark. Stations, the broadcast will start in fifteen minutes."

That happens again at 6:20 p.m. At 6:25 p.m., they count down by the minute from five minutes on. At 6:30 p.m., they play the prerecorded pregame opening.

During a men's basketball game in Norman, Oklahoma, we were working with a first-time board op in the studio in Oklahoma City.

We depend on the board op to count down to the last minute. I was keeping track of the time, and while we waited, I visited with John Thornton, the color analyst for that game.

As the teams warmed up, a ball came flying between us. I asked John if he had ever caught a ball in the face when he was coaching, and he said no.

I told a story about a game I worked in El Paso where I got hit right in the face. It knocked my headset off, my glasses went flying, and it cut the bridge of my nose. I explained how much it hurt.

Then I glanced down at my watch and saw that we were way past the time to go on the air. The board op can talk to the talent without the radio audience hearing him, so I asked, "Are we on the air?" He said yes.

I was caught flat-footed. All I could say was "Welcome to Lloyd Noble Arena. Tonight, the Aggies and the Oklahoma Sooners, and we will be back with the coach in a moment."

When we went to break, I asked the board op, "Did it dawn on you that we did not know we were live?"

"No," he said. "I thought it was just one of the strangest pregames I had ever heard."

I bet the listeners did too.

## MEMORY MOMENT
# 2017 Arkansas Game

On each of the broadcasts during my final football season, I shared a memory moment from a previous year. This one was used in the game at AT&T Stadium when we played Arkansas.

Last Saturday night, Mike Lednecky sent me a picture of the broadcast crew from Kansas. The Jayhawks were playing at Ohio University. The visiting radio booth was the office of the tight-ends coach at Ohio. The Kansas crew used the coach's desk for the broadcast gear and broadcast the game from a window that opened to the football field.

Let me say here that Kyle Field had two good radio booths in the old press box and has equally good booths in the new press box.

However, down through the years, visiting radio is often last on the list for space assignments from which to broadcast a game.

In 2007, at the Orange Bowl in Miami, we were *on top* of the stadium. We hauled the radio equipment up two flights of stairs only to find a space that looked like an unfinished duck blind. It was a wood frame made of two-by-fours with no walls. It did have a roof and a plywood table. We were up so high that seagulls actually flew below us!

In one stadium, we climbed a spiral staircase, pushing and pulling our 4′ × 4′ equipment box that weighed close to 100 pounds. The booth had a vent in the roof, and you could see the sky, but fortunately, I don't remember it ever raining.

One booth Dave Elmendorf and I worked in was just wide enough for the two of us to stand in. There was no room for any of our spotters, and the engineer set up in the hallway. Another broadcast booth lacked a door; instead, a tarp was hung across the doorway like a shower curtain.

Over 32 seasons, our broadcast team coped with water pipes, cement pillars, windows that wouldn't open, and power outlets that didn't work.

While we might've felt a lack of love for visiting radio on the road, we always felt the love at Kyle Field over our working conditions.

## More Radio Booth Memories

Radio booths across the country vary in their design. Sometimes the windows open, and sometimes they don't. Most if not all broadcasters like the window to be open. All of us feed off the crowd whether we are at home or on the road, and that aids in our enthusiasm in reporting the game.

A closed booth with a crowd mic plugged into the PA system just doesn't do the job. It's a very sterile atmosphere, and you don't get the effect of the fans cheering for their team.

Another aspect of booth design is the walls on either side of you. Some walls are painted, and you have no idea who is in the next booth. Other booths have glass walls, and you can see anything from fans in a luxury suite to the opposing team's radio announcers.

Some of you will remember the 2003 Texas A&M–Virginia Tech game in Blacksburg, Virginia. We played it on the edge of Hurricane Isabel and lost, 35–19. It was raining so hard that I asked Chris Valetta, a former player and our sideline announcer, to do his reporting in the radio booth. The window to my left was at the end of the press box. The stadium was old, and that window could not keep out much of the rain. When the game ended, we were standing in one inch of water.

Most announcers have all sorts of papers that we tape to the wall or window. These include the broadcast format, game notes, weather, standings, and games across the conference that day—in other words, items that are important for the broadcast.

Obviously, when we tape those papers to a window, they can block our view of the booth next to us. That was the case in Austin one year at Darrell K. Royal Memorial Stadium.

This window was about two feet wide and went all the way to the ceiling. I had taped notes that day that went a good six feet up the window. The only opening was about six inches above the countertop.

Through the opening, we only saw the weathered hands of the person sitting next to the window in the VIP booth for the Texas athletic department. The right hand was drawing a play on a napkin. Leanne was working this game with me, and she was watching the play as it was being outlined. She slowly peeled back a small part of one of my notes to see who it was.

She looked back and said I'd never guess who was drawing the play. It was Darrell Royal. He was drawing up the play and talking to the person sitting next to him: Tom Landry. She wanted to go over after the game to see if she could find that napkin, but it was gone.

The stadiums with broadcast booths that placed the radio crews from each school side by side would have been an interesting study for some psychology student. When you're winning, your booth is a New Year's Eve party. When you're losing, it's a morgue filled with long faces and blank stares.

Either way, winning or losing, I tried never to look over at the other announcers. I've been on both sides of that fence.

# 2017 Auburn Game

This memory moment salutes someone who works behind the microphone and a group of people who worked behind the scenes.

Dave Elmendorf sits to my right here in the radio booth. He is not only the color commentator on the Aggie radio broadcasts but also a good friend with a strong Christian walk.

As you have probably heard me say, Dave, class of '71, was a football All-American, a baseball All-American, an academic All-American, and a member of so many halls of fame that time does not allow me to mention them all.

Dave enjoyed a nine-year NFL career with the then–Los Angeles Rams, earning All-Pro twice and playing in the 1980 Super Bowl.

His insight is second to none. He never second-guesses, doesn't criticize the coaches or the players, and loves the Aggies. You can always count on Dave to say the right thing. No one could ask for a better broadcast partner than Dave Elmendorf.

Next are three men who have served or are serving the Aggie football broadcast with a very important position—booth engineer. These three had and have the responsibility of setting up the radio equipment to get the games on the air. It's not always that easy. Sometimes finding the right line connections is almost impossible, and then there are the times when the connection is dropped, and they get busy on the reconnect. These three are the first to arrive before the game and the last to leave when it ends. The first booth engineer was Ed Hadden, who worked for more than 20 years before retiring. His position was filled by Andrew Hicks, who works all home games, and Randy South, who works on the road.

Thank you to Ed, Andrew, and Randy for a job well done.

The next group I want to salute are the individuals who have served as sports information directors during my tenure in Aggieland.

The first is a well-known name in College Station, Tom Turbiville, whom I first met when he worked with the Southwest Conference (SWC). Later, after Tom left Texas A&M, he served as a sideline reporter on these broadcasts.

The second, Johnny Keith, came from Oklahoma and took over the position in the late 1980s. One of his assistants is now the current associate athletic director for media relations, Alan Cannon, but most of us who work with him know him as "AC."

Ask any member of the media who has been around for any time at all, and they will tell you that AC is simply the best. He has a great staff, and they do an outstanding job.

As a testament to the respect of his peers, it was just a short three years ago that Alan was voted into the College Sports Information Directors Hall of Fame.

Thank you to Tom, Johnny, and Alan (and his crack sports media team) for all they have done and still do to make these radio broadcasts better.

## MEMORY MOMENT
# 2017 UCLA Game

**Prior to the start of the Texas A&M–UCLA game in Pasadena, the first football game of my last season as the Texas A&M radio play-by-play announcer, I read the following two pieces in the pregame segment.**

Now I want to recognize those who worked as a part of the radio crew in the radio booth during the last 32 years. My apologies for any who I may leave out.

The current crew includes the following:
Dave Elmendorf
Will Johnson
Randy South

Andrew Hicks
Bob Davis
Mike Lednecky
Byran Farris
Bill Cross
Ed Hadden (the original engineer for well over 20 years)
Roger Lewis (the first booth producer)

Others who have been with us include the following:
Tom Dore
Jay Howard
Donnie Duncan
Tim Cassidy
Kevin Smith
Tim Stanfield
Brian Pendergraf
Jeff MacDonald
Tom Moyes
Mamie Elmendorf
Lori South
Dave Nelson
Matt Shillinglaw
Jim Benson
Gary Finkleman
John Appuliese
Chris Valetta
Tom Turbiville
George Jacobus
Ben Wall
Dawn Dickenson
Erin Jones
Bobby Jordan
Shane Elder

I hate to say it, but other names have slid off the page and disappeared over time. That is not to say that each of them did not contribute. To all these men and women, I say thank you.

On this first broadcast of my last season here in the football radio booth, I have had a request to go back from time to time in these pregames and talk about special moments. The first will be my first game ever as the designated announcer for Texas A&M football.

The Aggies would start with a Southeastern Conference (SEC) opponent that year and finish with an SEC team. Texas A&M traveled to Legion Field in Birmingham, Alabama, to take on the Alabama Crimson Tide. It would match then–Texas A&M head coach Jackie Sherrill against his alma mater.

Before 74,697 fans, the Tide would win 23–10. Kevin Murray would go 13 of 20 for 158 yards and no touchdowns. Craig Stump would see action as quarterback, hitting 6 of 7 for 51 yards. Alabama held a 10–3 lead at halftime. The Aggies would tie it up in the third quarter only to see the Tide score 13 unanswered points in the fourth.

It was a tough night running the ball, as Anthony Toney would carry for 58 yards and Roger Vick 36 yards. That would turn into a very dynamic one-two punch over the course of the season.

That 1985 game would mark the first time the Aggies had played Alabama since Coach Gene Stallings's Aggies had beaten his old head coach Bear Bryant's Crimson Tide in the 1968 Cotton Bowl. The 1985 match is still the only game played between the two in Birmingham.

The 1985 Aggie team would lose only two games that year going 10–2. They would capture the SWC championship and then beat Bo Jackson and Auburn in the Cotton Bowl 36–16.

Little did any of us know that year that the Aggies would move from the SWC in 1996 to the Big 12 and then to the SEC in 2012.

For me, it would be the start of a career that would allow me to see more Texas A&M sporting events in football, basketball, and baseball than anyone in the history of the school and, on top of that, to call games in all three conferences that the Aggies have called home. Let's all join together and have a great season and support these young men in maroon and white.

## Good Advice about Announcing Injuries

In this book, there is a story about the Exxon SWC radio network and its coverage of the football games in that league.

The network had a very thick rule book. One rule that absolutely had to be followed was to not mention any injury. If a player had to be carried off the field and did not return, you just simply did not mention it. If you were listening, you weren't told why Billy or little Johnny was no longer playing.

Network officials were afraid of how a family member might react if the broadcasters reported that the player had a broken leg or some other type of serious injury.

That rule came flying back to me one Saturday afternoon at Kyle Field. The halftime show featured the Aggie band and the alumni band. During the performance, a member of the alumni band collapsed on the field.

Everything stopped, and EMS personnel rushed out to help. In the broadcast booth, we had no idea what was wrong or what the band member's name was. We made the decision to close the window and look for members of the media to join us as guests. We said that the halftime would run longer due to performances by both the Aggie band and the alumni band.

Our decision came from my Exxon network days. There could have been family members listening who had someone marching that day. We didn't want to upset anyone because of our lack of information.

The good news was that the man had family there that day, and he did recover, which we would report sometime in the fourth quarter.

## The Coaches' Radio Shows

One of my responsibilities was hosting the coaches' radio shows.

Coach Jackie Sherrill had the first show, and it was carried live on television at the KAMU studio on campus. We took live calls, and the coach would field all questions.

We moved away from televising the radio show and moved it to a local restaurant. The *R. C. Slocum Show* started out at Chili's on Texas Avenue. RC Cola sponsored the show. R. C. had a great following from the Aggie students. One group called themselves the R. C. Pit Crew, and they were there every week.

The show would later move to Wings 'N More across from the campus golf course and then to the restaurant's new location on University Drive.

All the coaches' shows are currently hosted at Rudy's BBQ on Harvey Road.

Occasionally things got uncomfortable. Two ladies attending the Billy Gillispie Show almost came to blows. I have no idea what started the argument, but it got heated before friends stepped in and stopped it.

Another time, one lady asked if Coach Gillispie would ever hold a "basketball 101 for women" program so they could learn more about the game. He said no. They had tried that when he was in El Paso, and it turned out to be nothing more than some ladies trying to find him a wife. Then Billy added that if they held such an event, the women attending would think they knew more about the game than the coaches.

She replied, "I can see why you're not married."

One time during a coaches' show, a man yelled at some people in the back of the restaurant to quiet down. The response was not polite, and once again, cooler heads had to step in to separate two fellows who charged one another. I left the show at 8:00 p.m. that night and drove to campus to speak to the Fellowship of Christian Athletes. That was quite a contrast.

I would get to the show at 5:00 p.m., and we would start at 7:00 p.m. Before the football coaches' show one night, I noticed a man sitting at the end of the bar with a drink. He filled out a question card and laid it on the stack of cards on the broadcast table.

When the show ended, he had another drink in his hand and approached me. He asked why I didn't use his question. I asked which one was his. He went through the stack and handed me the card. It had been covered up by other questions, and we didn't have time for his as well as several others.

He said all I did was ask softball questions. I replied that it was the coaches' show and not the "Dave South Drills the Aggie Coach Show." For a few fleeting seconds, I thought he was going to throw his drink in my face, but he turned away instead.

# 3

# The Coaches

One part of my career at Texas A&M that I genuinely enjoyed was the relationship I had with the coaches in my three sports. I always had a good working relationship with each of them. In football, I worked with Jackie Sherrill, R. C. Slocum, Dennis Franchione, Mike Sherman, and Kevin Sumlin.

R. C., of course, spent 14 years as the Aggie head football coach. Due to the length of his career, we spent time together on the TV show, a weekly call-in radio show, postgame interviews, and pregame interviews. The night of the New Mexico game in 2017, I was honored that he presented me with a framed jersey in a pregame ceremony for the honorary team captain.

The coach and I had a common interest in music. I would share many selections from my personal library with him long after he left the coach's office.

Coach Sherrill was responsible for bringing me on board in 1985. I came to respect the fact that he was always looking for ways to make something better. Jackie is responsible for a live television call-in show. It was the first of its kind in the SWC. His success made Texas A&M a school to be respected on the gridiron. He sought to bring the culture of Texas A&M University into the football program, which drew fans even closer to what happened at Kyle Field each Saturday.

I never found that common denominator with Dennis Franchione. I enjoyed being around him, but it was rare that we engaged in deep conversation.

Mike Sherman was as good at evaluating talent as any coach I ever observed. He had certain standards that had to be met by any young man who wanted to play football at Texas A&M. If those standards weren't met, then the scholarship was not offered. Mike, like Kevin Sumlin, had been on staff with R. C. Slocum, and we had started our relationship then.

Kevin Sumlin and I had a great time on the Monday night radio show, and he made my job there as smooth as anything I've ever done on radio. R. C., Mike, and Kevin had a great sense of humor, which is something that I believe helps get you through life.

In my 48 years in college athletics, I always felt that every coach I worked with, whether at Texas A&M or elsewhere, knew they could trust me. I never for a minute considered writing a tell-all book that seems to be popular in some quarters.

My approach on the air was to just report what was happening down on the field without being negative. The score and statistics could convey to the listener that things were not going well.

## Aggie Basketball Coaches

In men's basketball, I worked with Shelby Metcalf, Kermit Davis, Tony Barone, Melvin Watkins, Billy Gillispie, Mark Turgeon, and Billy Kennedy.

Shelby was a legend among coaches. He coached a very physical game, and any opponent who took on the Aggies knew the games he coached would be wars. He was a reporter's dream because of his great one-liners, many of which were quoted in the newspapers and on the radio.

Kermit Davis spent just one season with the Aggies before some NCAA problems. That was disappointing because you could see that given time, he was going to put the program on top nationally. He would prove that at Middle Tennessee State and was just recently hired at Ole Miss.

Tony Barone and I hit it off right away. We traveled together, I shared family time with him and his bunch, and we both enjoyed baseball in the summer. Like Shelby, Tony coached hard-nosed basketball.

I was never sure why things did not work out at Texas A&M for Melvin Watkins. He was a good coach and had some good players, but nothing happened to push the team over the top.

Like my situation with Dennis Franchione, I never found a common denominator with Billy Gillispie. I will give him credit for making basketball popular again at Texas A&M. The crowds were there, and winning was back in style. Plus it was fun to broadcast the games.

The Aggies next turned to a young coach from Wichita State and a former Kansas player, Mark Turgeon. Mark picked up where Gillispie left off and spent four years with the program. The Aggies were in the NCAA's all four seasons and won 24-plus games each season. There was a real sense of loss when Mark left to go to Maryland. Mark was easy to work with, and those four seasons went by way too fast.

Some of us were concerned about who might replace Turgeon. To be honest, some of the names floating around as a possible replacement made me nervous.

All of us who knew Billy Kennedy when he was on the Kermit Davis staff were elated when Billy was named the next head coach. Billy, in my opinion, is a perfect fit for Texas A&M and our basketball program. Many people know that Billy was diagnosed with Parkinson's disease before he ever coached a game for the Aggies. Never did I hear Billy use that illness as any kind of excuse. What you saw in Billy in the public eye was exactly what I saw behind closed doors. Billy Kennedy, in this order, is a man of God, husband, father, and basketball coach. Billy embodies what a positive lifestyle is all about.

## Aggie Baseball Coaches

In baseball, there were just two coaches: Mark Johnson and Rob Childress.

Mark spent most of his career at Texas A&M and the last few years at Sam Houston State. Mark would win more than 1,000 games, which says a lot about his coaching career. I was deeply disappointed, as were a lot of Aggies, that Mark retired from Sam Houston State rather than Texas A&M.

Mark and I are in a group that meets once a week for coffee, and as always, I enjoy his company. We share the same thoughts about our spiritual lives, family, children, and grandchildren. We also share the same birthday, August 8.

Rob Childress, even though I am old enough to be his father, is like a younger brother to me. Rob loves what he does, and it shows in the results we have been getting with Aggie baseball.

Baseball has always been my favorite sport to broadcast, and Rob makes it easy to work with him, his coaches, and the team. Rob expects all who work with the program to be "all in," including the radio broadcasters.

I'm approaching the baseball broadcast on a year-to-year basis. I will be 73 years old when the 2019 season starts, so things like my health, my voice, my eyesight, and possible other factors will determine when I should step back.

I have never seen Rob let yesterday's win or yesterday's loss affect the next game on the schedule. That approach can also be seen in Rob's players.

The coaches in each of the sports always made me feel a part of the team. The fact that I was presented with 22 championship rings supports that feeling of being on a team.

Coaches, I was with you win or lose, but the winning was always more fun.

## Alan Weddell

Alan Weddell came to Texas A&M to work on the staff of head coach R. C. Slocum.

Following the 2002 season, then-Texas A&M president Dr. Robert Gates dismissed R. C. and his staff.

R. C. served as head coach from 1989 to 2002, longer than any coach in the history of the school. His record was 123–47–2. That was more wins than any Aggie coach dating back to the first season in 1894.

During those years, I became friends with many of the assistants and enjoyed those relationships.

Alan had played college football at the University of Texas but grew to love A&M and the Aggie fans. As I was walking off the field after the honorary captain recognition in 2017, there was Alan Weddell. That came as no surprise, as he was a regular at Aggie games at home and on the road.

The day the staff was dismissed in 2002, I was in my office in the Koldus Building when Alan walked in. He closed the door, sat down in the chair across from me, and didn't say anything for a minute or so—he just looked at me.

Then he said, "This is all your fault." I looked at him and asked how it was my fault.

"People believe everything you say," he said. "If you had said that we won all those games that we lost, they would have believed you, and we would still have our jobs!"

Good coach and a good sense of humor!

## The 2011 Florida State Super Regional

Earlier, I mentioned the two baseball coaches that I worked with at Texas A&M who are good men and good friends: Mark Johnson and Rob Childress.

Mark Johnson served as the Aggie head skipper for 21 years. His teams won three SWC Championships and two Big 12 regular season championships and went to the College World Series in 1993 and 1999.

Rob took over for Mark in 2005. Under his guidance, the Aggies have gone to the NCAA postseason tournament for 12 straight years; won a Big 12 regular season championship, three tournament championships, and one SEC tournament championship; and have gone to the College World Series in 2011 and 2017.

Mark was one of the first people to reach out to Rob and his family when they moved to College Station, inviting the Childress family to dinner in their home.

Rob led the way to get two jerseys hung on the fence at Olsen Field— one with Mark's number and the other with the number of former head coach Tom Chandler. One hangs down the left field line and the other hangs down the right.

Both Mark and Rob have a wonderful sense of humor. That is needed due to the length of the season and the ups and downs of baseball. One night your team might pitch a one-hit shutout and win and the next night lose 10–2. You must recover quickly because the team is playing four games a week.

Here's an example of that humor, which happened at the 2011 Florida State Super Regional. The Aggies had won the NCAA Regional at Olsen Field and traveled to the Super Regional in Tallahassee to take on legendary coach Mike Martin and a good Florida State team. The first night, the Aggies won 6–2. The Aggie starter Ross Stripling went seven innings, allowing seven hits, two runs, and one walk while striking out eight.

The Aggies lost game two in a blow-out and then came back to take game three behind Aggie pitcher Michael Wacha, who went 7.1 innings, only allowing three hits and two runs and striking out eight. That win sent the Aggies to the College World Series.

Now back to game two. After four rather ugly innings, the Aggies were down 10–0. Jason Hutchins, a former player and now the director of operations for baseball, was standing by Coach Childress. Jason said Coach Childress looked up at the press box and then looked at him and said, "I wonder what Dave is talking about?"

## The Charlie Moran Story

Not long after I started with Texas A&M in 1985, I was asked to narrate the "History of Aggie Football." The video was a project started by athletics director and head football coach Jackie Sherrill.

The video script was well researched and well written with historic pictures, interviews, and video. It really helped me on the air, since I was only two years deep into my work with Aggie football.

The story about Charles B. Moran caught my attention. Coach Moran (nicknamed "Uncle Charley") gained fame as a catcher and umpire in Major League Baseball. He also coached at Texas A&M, Carlisle, Bucknell, Centre College, and Catawba, as well as the Frankford Yellow Jackets.

Moran was born in 1878 in Nashville, Tennessee, and died in 1949 at the age of 71. How many people do you know who took their final breath in Horse Cave, Kentucky?

He played football for Tennessee in 1897 and then at Bethel College in Tennessee in 1898 and 1899. He would surface again in 1903 and 1908, playing baseball for the St. Louis Cardinals.

He took up umpiring in the National League in 1918 and stayed in the league until 1939. He worked the World Series in 1927, 1929, 1933, and 1938.

Back to Texas A&M and the start of Moran's coaching career with the Aggies. There is no reason given, but he was elevated from an assistant's position to head coach after the second game in 1909, his first year in College Station.

His record with the Aggies was 38–8–4, but since the Aggies did not join the SWC until 1915, Moran never coached a conference football game. In 1915, A&M's first year in the SWC, Moran was replaced by E. H. Harlan.

In those six years, only four other Aggie coaches had a better winning percentage than Moran. Those four, however, coached no more than two years. Moran's .800 winning percentage is best in A&M history based or three or more years as an Aggie head coach.

If we use five years as the minimum to be the head coach to rank winning percentages, the top three are Charlie Moran (.800 percent), D. X. Bible (.768 percent), and R. C. Slocum (.721 percent).

Now here's a fact that Aggie fans should love about Uncle Charley Moran: Texas A&M played Texas in 1909, 1910, and 1911 but not in 1912, 1913, or 1914. The Longhorns pop back up on the schedule in 1915, when E. H. Harlan took over.

What happened? It seems Texas accused Moran of playing dirty football and refused to play the Aggies if he was the Aggie head coach. A&M countered by saying that Texas was using ineligible players. The Texas students disliked Moran so much that they sang a song that went like this: "To hell, to hell with Charley Moran and all his dirty crew, and if you don't like the words of this song, to hell, to hell with you."

With Moran gone in 1915, the two would resume the series and play every year until 2011, when A&M left to join the SEC.

(Some notes in this story were found on Wikipedia.)

# Dave's Take

## Athletics Conferences, the SWC Radio Network, and Memorabilia

### The Southwest Conference

I grew up in Wichita Falls and with the SWC. Many of my friends from Wichita Falls went to Texas Tech, Texas, and some went to Texas A&M.

In tracing the history of the SWC, you will find that for 82 years, from 1914 to the spring of 1996, the SWC had avid fans and a competitive race each year in football and basketball. At one time or another, the following 13 different schools were members of the SWC:

University of Arkansas, 1915–1991
Baylor University, 1915–1996
University of Houston, 1972–1996 (Olympic sports, 1972;
    football, 1976)
University of Oklahoma, 1915–1919
Oklahoma A&M University (now Oklahoma State), 1915–1925
Phillips University (Enid, Oklahoma; the school closed in the late
    1990s), 1920
Rice University, 1915–1996
Southern Methodist University (SMU), 1918–1996

Southwestern University (Georgetown, Texas), 1915–1916
Texas Christian University, 1923–1996
University of Texas, 1915–1996
Texas A&M University, 1915–1996
Texas Tech University, 1956–1996

Other leagues were signing big television contracts while the SWC was left standing beside the road with a big revenue shortfall from television dollars.

The SWC got complacent and didn't pay attention to the changes happening with the fan base. The professional game was getting stronger in the state of Texas and drawing fans away from conference schools.

Major League Baseball, the National Football League, the National Basketball Association, and even professional hockey had moved into the state. Television coverage and big advertising dollars followed these professional entities.

There were two teams that were the drawing cards for fans and television, Texas A&M and Texas, with a third being Texas Tech. In later years, the others, as members of other leagues, would start to attract television and sponsorships.

A major accomplishment in the early days was the creation of the Humble SWC Radio Network, which started in 1936. It later became the Exxon SWC Radio Network. Each school received an equal revenue distribution for football, but in 1974, Exxon lost the contract. According to A&M athletic department officials, Exxon paid each school $15,000 per season.

The new network that took over in 1973 paid $25,000 per school and gave equal distribution every Saturday for every team and all games. This meant that an SWC game would air every Saturday, and every SWC team would have the same number of games broadcast over the radio network.

Texas A&M, Texas, and Arkansas wanted more. They wanted all their games on the radio every Saturday during football season. Athletics director and head football coach Jackie Sherrill took the lead in fighting for more revenue and a network for Texas A&M. Jackie was successful, and A&M soon had its games on 50-plus stations. Texas would have a network of 30-plus stations. Arkansas had the Razorback State to itself.

*Coach Jackie Sherrill and me on the set of the Jackie Sherrill Show in about 1986 or 1988. The show was recorded on Saturday night following the games. There was a time when we also accepted phone calls with questions for the coach. The show was recorded in the KAMU television studios on the Texas A&M campus.*

*Coach R. C. Slocum (seated, fourth from left) and me on the set of his show, along with some of our crew.*

*This is one of the last pictures of Andrew Hicks, Dave Elmendorf, and me in the new broadcast booth at Kyle Field. Andrew served as our engineer after Ed Hadden retired. Andrew also engineered the coaches' shows for football and basketball.*

*Anthony Ware played basketball for Texas A&M in 1991 and 1992. In this photo, he had come back for an Aggie basketball reunion during the 2017–2018 basketball season. Anthony was one of my favorite players, and I got to meet his lovely family at the reunion. It is always a thrill to visit with former players and their families when they come back to campus.*

*For my 70th birthday in 2015, Leanne and I hosted a birthday party at the Wings 'N More restaurant in College Station. Much like some of the coaches' shows, we hosted a trivia contest and gave away prizes! It was a fun celebration with family, friends, neighbors, and athletic department coworkers.*

*This a picture of the backstop at Bridwell Park in Wichita Falls, the first baseball field I ever played on. It was also the scene of a loss I will never forget. My 12-year-old team, the Texacos, lost to our bitter rival, the Giants. James Star hit a line drive that was caught by the second baseman, and I was doubled-off second. To this day, that loss still hurts!*

*The Famous Bus 12. Its builder, Keith Lane, once utilized the train tracks beside the baseball stadium for one of the more creative Aggie Yell Leader campaign stunts ever attempted. He didn't win the election, but his Aggie spirit remains undimmed, as shown by his later construction of Bus 12.*

*This is the 2013 Cotton Bowl Crew. Texas A&M, led by Heisman-winning quarterback Johnny Manziel, beat Oklahoma, 41–13. Left to right: Jim Benson, Bob Davis, Dave Elmendorf, me, Dr. Ed Richards, Mike Lednicky, Todd Starnes, Andrew Hicks, Byran Farris, and Ryan Janek.*

*Damon Johnson, just like Anthony Ware, was another one of my favorite Aggie basketball players. You could always count on Damon to give you all he had from opening tip to final buzzer. He lettered from 1992 to 1995.*

*My last home game for Aggie football was the 2017 win against New Mexico, which the Aggies won 55–14. Lindsey Quisenberry from the Letterman's Association escorted my family onto the field when I was recognized as the honorary team captain. Part of the ceremony included the presentation of a framed 12th Man jersey presented by former head coach R. C. Slocum.* (Photo courtesy of the Texas A&M Letterman's Association)

This is a shot of my office at the "old" Kyle Field. My office had been the football trainer's office in the old locker room located underneath the west-side bleachers. I did all my game recording and game prep there. At one time or another, I had offices at G. Rollie White, the Koldus Building, this space at Kyle Field, and at Blue Bell Park. This was my favorite spot. You could walk straight to the football field and enter at the 50-yard line.

A fun broadcast I was involved with before every home game at Kyle Field was the Fan Zone. The booth was set up in the north end zone area where we visited with Aggie fans, interviewed special guests, and talked about the upcoming game. In this photo, I'm sitting next to cohost Scott Clendenin (pictured here on my right). To my left is Rick Hall, a longtime football official, whom we interviewed at the beginning of each season about upcoming rule changes. He and his wife, Mel, are also our next-door neighbors.

The NCAA Tournament in Oklahoma City in 2016. The four of us are all play-by-play announcers with Learfield Sports. Left to right: Toby Rowland, University of Oklahoma; Robby Robinson, Virginia Commonwealth University; and Gary Rima, Northern Iowa University.

It was always nice to run into former players and catch up on their lives after Texas A&M. I ran into these three at a 2017 Texas Sports Hall of Fame: SWC Hall of Fame event in Fort Worth. Left to right: James Brooks (1994–1995), me, LeeLand McElroy (1993–1995), and Alcie Peterson (1994–1995).

*My granddaughter, Gianna, has been
attending Aggie basketball games since
she was a newborn! As she got older, it
became customary for her to come see me
during the halftime of an Aggie men's
home game.*

*Another picture from the honorary captain ceremony at my last home game at Kyle
Field. Grub Burger general manager Chase Redpath presented me with a game ball.
Grub Burger was a Texas A&M Ventures corporate sponsor.* (Photo courtesy of
The Texas A&M Letterman's Association)

*Many of you have heard the story of my being thrown out of a basketball game at the 1993 SWC tournament. That story is included in this book. In that story, I mention Matt Menzl, the announcer for Wisconsin-Green Bay, who had the same experience. This is a picture of Matt and me in Oklahoma City at the 2016 NCAA basketball tournament.*

*In December 2017, I received the Ron Stone Award by the Touchdown Club of Houston. This photo shows my family and friends, who joined us for this wonderful event. Starting on the left and going clockwise: Leanne, Harry and Shirley Lewis, Melanie and Eddy Boyd, Jack Caltagirone, Lori South, and Gianna South*

*The 2017 Belk Bowl was my last Aggie football broadcast. After the game, four of us went back to the hotel for dinner. Wake Forest won the game 55–52, which meant the Aggies lost the first game and the last game of my last season with Texas A&M football. Left to right: Byran Farris, me, Randy South, and Mike Lednicky*

At the 2018 SEC Tournament in St. Louis, I got to meet Jim Nantz of CBS Sports. He is a class act and understandably admired by his fellow broadcasters and fans across the country.

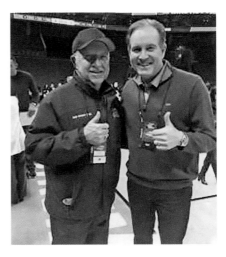

You would be hard pressed to meet an older Aggie who did not know about the Junction Boys. I have gotten to know many of them down through the years and heard their stories about their experiences. The training camp they used is now a part of Texas Tech Junction. This is one of the barracks the team used. It was a screened-in cabin with no air conditioning and wooden shutters that were lowered in case of rain.

Starting with Jackie Sherrill through Kevin Sumlin, I hosted the coach's radio shows at two different restaurants. When Billy Gillispie came on board, we added a basketball coach's show. This is Coach Billy Kennedy at Rudy's BBQ in College Station.

One of my dearest friends is Colin Killian. Colin was our sports information director for basketball and a color analyst for the road games. Colin, at this writing, is the public communications manager for the City of College Station. The occasion for this picture was when he asked to me speak to a group of College Station volunteers.

I'm not sure who took this picture, but it shows the radio crew walking out of the stadium at the Belk Bowl in Charlotte, North Carolina, after the game. Randy South, our engineer on the road, is in the lead, Dave Elmendorf is in the black jacket, and I'm wearing the maroon jacket. It was my last walk out of a football stadium as an Aggie radio broadcaster.

In this book, you will find the story of Corporal Matthew Bradford, USMC (retired). This picture was taken during the pregame show from Rupp Arena in Lexington, Kentucky. Matt did the scouting report on Kentucky.

My basketball broadcast partner Al Pulliam was doing the Aggie scouting report as this was taken.

*Mike Caruso and me during a broadcast of an Aggie basketball game against Auburn. Someone took a shot of a television when we were flashed up during the telecast. Mike did a lot of the road games over the last three or four years when Al Pulliam had other responsibilities in his work with Texas A&M Foundation.*

*We lost a great man and a great baseball player when Wally Moon passed on February 9, 2018. Wally lettered in baseball at Texas A&M in 1949 and 1950 and then went on to a stellar 12-year major-league career with the St. Louis Cardinals and the Los Angeles Dodgers. On two different occasions, I interviewed Wally for the Fan Zone and for the baseball broadcast. He was a wealth of knowledge and played during a time when I was starting to fall in love with the game. There is a Wally Moon Gold Glove on display at Dodger Stadium on Los Angles.*

*This is 95-year-old Julie Martin visiting Rick Hill (the voice of Blue Bell Park) and me in 2016. Julie is a great fan of Aggie baseball, and when she can't attend a game, she listens on the radio! Julie was born in Waco and grew up in Houston before moving to College Station.*

*This is the crew that worked the 2017 Ole Miss game that the Aggies won 31–24. Left to right: Gary Finkelman, Dave Elmendorf, me, Zach Barrett, and John Appuliese*

*Rarely do I get to tailgate, but when Leanne and I drove our motor home to Hoover, Alabama, for the 2018 SEC baseball tournament, we made up for lost time! There is an RV park with 170 sites right next to the ballpark, and we walked back and forth to the games. We parked next to Ole Miss fans, and every night we were invited to join a group of 30-plus Rebel fans for some great food and fun conversation. For those Aggies who like to drive their RVs to Aggie events, the SEC baseball tournament and the Hoover RV park should be on your Aggie bucket list.*

*For most bowl games, we did a prebowl show from the team hotel. That was the case in this picture. I was interviewing Andy Richardson, who heads up 12th Man Productions for Texas A&M Athletics. Right above me is engineer Ed Hadden and then Dave Elmendorf, who was cohosting the show.*

*My last home game at Kyle Field in 2017. Former head coach R. C. Slocum has just presented me with a framed 12th Man jersey. To my left is Chase Redpath representing Aggie corporate sponsor Grub Burger, who had just given me a game ball. The jersey is now on display at Rudy's BBQ in College Station. Our granddaughter, Gianna, now has the game ball at her home.* (Photo courtesy of the Letterman's Association)

*During my 32 years with the Aggies, the teams that I worked with (football, basketball, baseball) won a collective total of 22 championships. Each time a team won a championship, I was among those who, along with the team, received a championship ring. Those 22 rings are on display at Aggieland Credit Union on Southwest Parkway in College Station.*

*My last first game was a thrill as the Aggies played UCLA in the Rose Bowl. That meant I got to broadcast games from the Rose Bowl, Cotton Bowl, Sugar Bowl, and Orange Bowl. I would only miss the Fiesta Bowl. The Aggies lost to UCLA that day in a heartbreaker, 45–44, after being up 38–10 at halftime. A&M would score only six points in the second half.*

*This is a picture of former Aggie pitcher Ross Stripling. The other half of the Aggies' pitching dynamic duo from 2010 to 2012 was Michael Wacha. My son Randy and I were invited down on the field before a game at Dodger Stadium for this photo op. Michael and Ross are two former Aggie student athletes and quality young men.*

*Kevin Sumlin Radio Show at Rudy's BBQ in College Station. Occasionally, we would have a special guest. This night it was our granddaughter, Gianna.*

*In this picture, I am standing on Olsen Field with former players who came back for an "Old Timers" game. Next to me is a former player and my friend Scott Smith. Scott and I attend Central Baptist Church in College Station. We attended his and Alyssa's wedding and enjoy watching them raise their two sons.*

*My broadcast partner for Aggie baseball is Scott Clendenin, a former Texas A&M student. Scott's love and knowledge of Aggie baseball shines through on the radio when he is on the air.*

*The Kevin Sumlin Radio Show at Rudy's BBQ in College Station. Kevin and I did 12 shows per season plus a bowl show. Kevin was a great guy to work with and a great talker, which made my job easy!*

*All broadcasters depend on a lot of help to prepare for every game. The Texas A&M sports media department, led by CoSIDA Hall of Famer Alan Cannon, is the best in the country, in my opinion. One member of that team is Thomas "TD" Dick, who works with Aggie baseball. TD provides me with all that I need to get the game on the air. He is also an avid reader and offers book reviews on his Facebook page.*

*Board ops are the young men and women who work at the studios during each broadcast. They insert the commercials and keep us on time. Some I never met, others I did. Travis Roberts, a University of Missouri graduate, started as our board op when he was still in high school. After spending time listening to Aggie football and basketball, Travis and his father drove to College Station to experience a gameday weekend in Aggieland.*

*An interesting project I got to be a part of was the Former Yell Leaders Association, which began in the early 1990s. I asked some the former Yell Leaders if they ever got together on a football weekend—they said no. I joined with Dick Biondi, and we started a campaign on the radio broadcast asking all former Yell Leaders to send us their current contact information. The group had its first gathering in 1994 at Red Cashion's cabin and has been meeting ever since. It's interesting how the yells have changed over the years. There were yells the older guys did that younger fellows had never heard of and vice versa. I enjoy attending these events to hear a lot of history and a lot of stories. This photo was with the 2017–2018 Yell Leaders during my last year with Aggie football and basketball. Left to right: Connor Joseph, Kenneth Belden, me, Ian Moss, Cooper Cox, and Gavin Suel.*

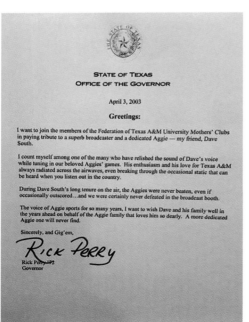

*When Linda Hill of the Texas A&M Mothers' Club dedicated the yearbook to me in 2003, I received this letter from then governor Rick Perry.*

STATE OF TEXAS
OFFICE OF THE GOVERNOR

April 3, 2003

**Greetings:**

I want to join the members of the Federation of Texas A&M University Mothers' Clubs in paying tribute to a superb broadcaster and a dedicated Aggie — my friend, Dave South.

I count myself among one of the many who have relished the sound of Dave's voice while tuning in our beloved Aggies' games. His enthusiasm and his love for Texas A&M always radiated across the airwaves, even breaking through the occasional static that can be heard when you listen out in the country.

During Dave South's long tenure on the air, the Aggies were never beaten, even if occasionally outscored...and we were certainly never defeated in the broadcast booth.

The voice of Aggie sports for so many years, I want to wish Dave and his family well in the years ahead on behalf of the Aggie family that loves him so dearly. A more dedicated Aggie one will never find.

Sincerely, and Gig'em,

*Rick Perry*

Rick Perry '72
Governor

*Having breakfast in July 2018 in College Station and look who I run into!*

*Former Texas governor Rick Perry, who was at the time of this meeting serving our great nation as the 14th United States secretary of energy.*

*September 22, 2001—the student-led fund-raising effort known as Red, White, and Blue Out. Texas A&M was playing Oklahoma State after 9/11. Fans in the bottom deck wore blue, those on the second deck wore white, and those on the third deck wore red. Those of us in the radio booth wore red. This effort raised $180,000, which went to relief funds for the New York City police and fire departments.*

*Tom Turbiville was the first sports information director I worked with at Texas A&M. Tom has been a major part of the Bryan–College Station community since those days in the athletic department. We've worked baseball together, and in this photo, we were about to do a game at Minute Maid Park in Houston. Tom is the radio voice for Texas A&M women's basketball.*

*Texas A&M played Pittsburgh at Heinz Field on September 7, 2002. The Aggies won the game in a low-scoring affair, 14–12. A year later at Kyle Field, Pittsburgh would win 37–26. What was challenging about Heinz Field was the radio booth. It was located at the side of the end zone, and we were looking back up the field at an angle. The booth was also too low to allow us to get any depth perception, so we had a real problem*

*determining the exact yard line. The same issue, to a lesser degree, exists in the radio booth at AT&T Stadium in Arlington. What saves the broadcast crew there is the gigantic video board.*

In 2001 and 2002, former Aggie All-American and Dallas Cowboy defensive back Kevin Smith worked as the color analyst on Aggie football games. He's one of the outstanding former players who would go on to the play for the Dallas Cowboys. Kevin lettered for the Aggies from '88 to '91. The 2003 season was filled by former associate athletic director Tim Cassidy, now at Arizona State.

Little Broadcaster Trent Hall, '15, is now in the United States Air Force. He and his brother Jesse are the sons of Rick and Mel Hall, our next-door neighbors.

Little Broadcaster Adam Dewitt, '14, lived on the other side of us from the Halls. His parents, Robbie and Cindy, have been our neighbors for more than 20 years.

Rosenblatt Stadium in Omaha, Nebraska, where I would broadcast Aggie CWS games in 1993 and 1999. The stadium was demolished when the games were moved to TD Ameritrade Park.

The other schools were struggling to build networks. One had fewer than a dozen, and most only had a station in their home market. The conference had reached a point of no return. Texas A&M's radio revenue went from $25,000 a year to $1 million a year overnight and then to five million and even more as time went by.

The bigger issue for the SWC was the scandals, which grew rampant during the 1980s. Every school except Rice, Baylor, and Arkansas was disciplined by the NCAA. SMU's football program was suspended for two years, after the sport was assessed the "death penalty." Texas A&M, at one point, was the most penalized school in NCAA history.

One weekend, I found out just how bad things had gotten. I was working an away game with two teams that will go unnamed. The format at this time called for pregame coach's interviews. I would go to the home team's practice on Friday and interview that coach and then go to the hotel of the visiting team to do that interview.

The second interview turned out to be the eye-opener. When the coach opened the door, he was in the bottom of the fifth, and we were not playing baseball. Nothing was recorded that evening as he talked and I listened. His team was having a bad year, and the prospects of it getting any better did not look good. All that he told me later came to light during NCAA investigations. He even predicted that SMU was headed for major trouble but did not mention the death penalty.

By 1991, Arkansas officials had had enough and announced that the school would withdraw and join the SEC. By 1996, merger talks started between SWC and the Big 8 that resulted in four teams from the SWC—Texas, Texas A&M, Texas Tech, and Baylor—joining teams from the Big 8 to create the Big 12 Conference.

Since the Aggies joined the Big 12 and then the SEC, I have not heard a hint of any wrongdoing. As far as Texas A&M is concerned, I believe it was the ethics, integrity, and character of the coaches that kept the Aggies on a straight path. I also salute former compliance director David Batson, who left in August 2018 to join the SEC office, for leading the way in building a model compliance program. He not only helped the coaches but also educated the fan base.

As a full-time employee starting in 1990, I had to sign a paper that said if I observed what I thought was an NCAA infraction, I had to report it, or I could be terminated. I would see the occasional minor infractions and report those but never experienced anything major.

I remember one Thanksgiving with my family at a local country club. One of our donors, his family, and one of our players were just a few tables away. At that time, believe it or not, that was a minor violation. I had to report it, since they saw me and I saw them. The player had to reimburse that donor for the cost of the meal.

As David Batson use to say, "Ask before you act!"

## The Southwest Conference Radio Network

Growing up in Texas, we listened to Southwest Conference Football on the radio. The games were first broadcast over the Humble Southwest Conference Radio Network and then over the Exxon Southwest Conference Radio Network.

I still have a framed patch that could be pinned to your brown network jacket to signify you were on the Exxon broadcast team. Why was it brown? No school in the conference had brown as a color. You were to remain neutral at all cost throughout every broadcast. If there was a hint that you were partial to a team, you would get a call on Monday. By the way, believe it or not, that never happened to me.

I became a homer only when the broadcast became the Texas A&M Sports Network. I never hid the fact that I wanted the Aggies to win, and that approach was expected of me.

The Humble Network went all out in their support of the SWC. You could fill up with gas and get a tumbler with each of the schools' logos on the side. There were bumper stickers, tiny little pennants, and even schedule cards. One year, there were nice paperweights, and I'm sure there were more items that I can't remember.

We would rehearse each broadcast about an hour and half out from kickoff, practicing the breaks and reading live copy. The broadcast equipment was a challenge. The network hired contract engineers, and each one had his own equipment. Normally, the equipment was anywhere from 10 to 20 years old, and much of which wasn't even sold in those days.

One time, the airline lost the equipment. Our engineer called local radio stations, borrowing anything they had. When we went on the air the next day, the microphone I used was hung around my neck, and the engineer used a coat hanger to make a mic holder. I wonder to this day what others in the press box thought about how I was wired.

As mentioned earlier, if a player was injured, you were not to mention it. Network officials feared that a relative back home might have a health problem if a son or grandson went out with an injury. The player just left the game and no reason was ever given. That rule came in handy years later during a game at Kyle Field.

The distribution of the games was important for each member school. Exxon made sure that every school had its games on the air across Texas in every major market. Even the small markets had games on the air. We spend our summer vacation in the Davis Mountains of West Texas. Most years I drove to Alpine to visit Ray Hendryx, the owner of KVLF radio. Ray and his dad before him had carried Aggie football since 1947. They started with the Humble Oil and Refinery Southwest Conference Radio Network.

The eye-opener for me was when I was told about the rights fees from the network to the schools. Today, rights fees are in the millions. In those days, according to what I was told, no school got more than $15,000 a year.

There were many good announcers who worked those games, but at the top of the list was Kern Tips. I never had the pleasure of meeting Tips because he retired before I started. When I announced my retirement at the end of the 2017 season, I was the last of the SWC Exxon announcers still broadcasting football.

## Five Things I Liked about the Three Conferences

Southwest Conference:

> The relationships with the sports staff from each school
> The short trips to play the games (could drive to all but Arkansas)
> The Southwest Conference Press Tour each summer (great
>    fellowship)
> Bo Carter, the longtime conference sports information director
>    (kind heart with an upbeat, funny personality)
> The Southwest Conference Radio Network (one of a kind)

The Big 12:

The relationships with the sports staff from each school
Downtown Lawrence, Kansas (lots to see and do)
The Bricktown Ballpark (Oklahoma City), home of the
    postseason baseball tournament (nice ballpark and walkable
    venue in downtown Oklahoma City)
The Big 12 Basketball Tournament (Kansas City; great
    atmosphere)
Allen Fieldhouse at the University of Kansas (historic basketball
    arena)

Southeastern Conference:

The welcome we received when Texas A&M entered the
    conference
The relationships with the sports staff from each school
The square in downtown Oxford, Mississippi (a must-visit)
The way the fans at each school support their teams (in all sports)
The Eagle at Auburn (a must-see pregame ceremony)
The SEC Baseball Tournament (great venue in Hoover, Alabama,
    with an outstanding fan fest and an RV park right next to the
    stadium)

Time and time again before we played our first SEC game in 2012 and throughout that first year of competition, fans made us feel welcome. The Aggies were playing in a basketball tournament at Madison Square Garden. Kentucky had played a game the night before against Kansas and won 75–65.

Some Wildcat fans were eating breakfast the morning after just a few tables away from where Al Pulliam and I were sitting. We were wearing Aggie warm-ups. The Kentucky fans got up from their table, came over, and told us how excited they were that Texas A&M was coming to the SEC.

That very thing happened several times with other SEC fans at other venues. We felt at home!

## DeWare Field House and Memorabilia

With all the changes in facilities over the years, I wanted to collect pieces from old sites that had been part of my career or part of the history of athletics at Texas A&M. Some of the memorabilia collected came courtesy of construction projects at Kyle Field and Olsen Field.

DeWare Field House was one of the first homes for Aggie basketball. It stood out in front of Kyle Field from 1924 to 1997. Basketball moved to G. Rollie White Coliseum in 1954, and the field house was torn down in 1997 during the Kyle Field north end zone project.

When DeWare was torn down, John Thornton and I went over and asked for a piece of the wall. They said we could have all we wanted. We each loaded up a section and took them home. My section is now the corner of the flower bed in our front yard.

I was mowing the yard one day when a car stopped, and the man driving got out. He pointed at the section of the wall and asked if it was a part of DeWare Field House. I said yes. He said he thought so, got back in the car, and drove away. To this day, I have no idea who he was.

Another keepsake is one of the original lights from Kyle Field. When they changed the lighting, they were sending the old ones to the scrapyard. I was able to get one, and we turned it into a large flower pot.

Two items that were thrown away, but that I was able to save, were the two lights from the old scoreboard shaped like footballs. These lights indicated who had possession of the football. My son Randy and I rewired both and each have one.

When the old horseshoe was torn down to make room for the Richardson Zone at Kyle Field (what I referred to earlier as the north end zone project), I was able to save part of a step that has the number of one of the aisles.

Finally, when the renovation started at Olsen Field to make way for Blue Bell Park, I added two more items to my collection. My broadcast location was out in front of the press box, and I sat under section numbers 210 and 211. These two numbers represented the section out in front of the broadcast booth.

# 5

# Fans

## Say (and Do) the Darndest (and Nicest) Things

Interacting with Aggies, Aggie fans, and fans from other schools was either a gratifying or a trying experience. Looking back now, I laugh about a few of the encounters with other schools' fans. Aggie fans, on the other hand, are the best. I will be forever grateful for their kindness and encouragement.

## The Aggies and the Broadcast

I had many opportunities to speak to Aggie groups across the state during my 32 years of announcing. It was always interesting to hear where and how Aggies listened to games on the radio.

●

An Aggie shrimper provided a good tale at a meeting in Houston. He was in his boat in the Gulf of Mexico zigzagging left to right. The boat had been going back and forth for about 20 minutes when someone broke the radio silence.

The voice on the radio said they had never seen shrimp move like this and wondered what the Aggie shrimper was doing. The Aggie looked out and saw some three or four shrimp boats on both the left and the right of his boat.

He went on the radio to tell them that he had pulled up his nets and turned off the sonar. Instead, he was trying to tune the radio to the Aggie football game!

●

Then there was the fire captain in one of our major cities. He told me that he and his men were fighting a big fire at an abandoned warehouse, with the A&M football game blaring out over the loudspeaker on the fire truck.

●

I've been told there was another Aggie who took his radio and earbuds to a wedding. In the middle of the service, he suddenly yelled out "Yes!" when the Aggies scored. He apparently got a slap on the leg from his wife, who was embarrassed by the outburst.

●

Finally—and this didn't come from an Aggie event—a couple in Pennsylvania emailed to say they listened to every game on the internet. In the spirit of the 12th Man, they stood in their living room for the entire broadcast.

## Fan-Friendly Kyle Field

When the press box was on the west side of Kyle Field, we were so close to the fans on the top row below us that we could reach out from our open window and shake hands.

Over time, Dave Elmendorf and I developed relationships with those folks. Every game, one of them would ask for a few line-up cards to pass out to nearby friends. Sometimes one of the ladies would bake cookies and pass them up to us. As we watched replays on the television monitor, several would turn around and wait for us to give them a thumbs up or down. During time-outs, we would talk to them about the game or answer questions about statistics or give our opinion about an official's call.

Many brought radios and listened to the broadcast even though they were right there in the stands. During one game there was a fellow standing up (no radio on), yelling at the coach, which was interesting, since he was on the third deck. Elmendorf was talking, so I took off my headset and listened to what he was saying.

When Elmendorf finished, I repeated what the guy had said about something he thought the coach should do. Dave immediately said that was the last thing the coach should do.

That was it! Dave Elmendorf was the authority. Three or four fans sitting nearby with radios started yelling at the guy. With a shocked look on this face, he turned around, looked at them, and then sat down.

Unless he was told after the game, he never knew the radio crew had thrown him under the bus.

## Dave Elmendorf and the Michigan Game

This story comes from one of our road trips to Baton Rouge when Texas A&M and LSU had renewed a home-and-home series during Jackie Sherrill's tenure as head coach, beginning in 1986. This happened somewhere in the early 1990s.

Dave Elmendorf was my broadcast partner for 26 years, serving as the color analyst on the games. Dave is a former player at Texas A&M. He was a football All-American, a baseball All-American, and an academic All-American. Dave went on to the NFL and spent nine years playing for the Los Angeles Rams (1971–1979).

Coming out of college, he was drafted by the Rams and by the New York Yankees and had to choose between pro football or pro baseball. Dave has represented Texas A&M in a positive way and is a great example and role model for our current players.

Anyway, Dave and I were sitting in the lobby of our hotel one morning before the LSU game that night. I happened to see an older gentleman walking in our direction using a cane (I need to mention here that Dave hadn't played at Texas A&M since 1971).

When it became apparent that the man was walking toward us, I stood up and walked over to meet him. I extended my hand and introduced myself. The gentleman said he knew who I was, had listened to Aggie broadcasts for years, and wanted to come over and say hello. I turned to introduce him to Dave, but when Dave extended his hand, the gentleman replied, "Yeah, I know who he is. He dropped the punt in the Michigan game!"

With that said, he turned around and walked away!

## First-Year SEC Lunch Bet

In 2012, the Aggies started to play in the SEC. It would be my third conference with Texas A&M and most likely the last move that A&M would make. There was a lot of excitement among the fans at the thought of joining the best conference in the country.

I'm part of a Friday lunch group made up of fellows from a men's Bible study at my church. One member of that group (let's call him Joe) is an Alabama graduate. In August, close to the start of the school year, Joe started to make some brash statements about Texas A&M's chances of competing in the SEC.

It started to wear a little thin, so one Friday, I told Joe that I thought the Aggies would win at least 8 games—maybe as many as 10. I also gave us a win at Tuscaloosa. Joe said that would never happen, so I bet him a steak dinner it would, and he accepted the bet.

The Friday before the Alabama game, the Aggies had seven wins, so the game with the Tide would be number eight. Joe was full of Alabama glory, telling us to get ready for a butt-kicking by the Crimson Tide.

I told Joe that the Aggies were going to win that game and earn their eighth win. I must've been full of Aggie maroon because I bet him a second steak dinner.

The score was Texas A&M 29–Alabama 24: Dave wins two steak dinners!

By the way, people have asked about the "lightning in a bottle" comment I made at the end of that game. I was riding from Birmingham to

Tuscaloosa with my friend and former yell leader Jim Benson. On the way over, we were listening to a science show (of all things) on the radio. One of the men talking said, "That would be like catching lightning in a bottle." I looked at Jim and told him that when we won today, that's what I was going to say. The Aggies won, and I said it!

## Kill 'Em with Kindness

One time, after a game, I was walking across the old parking lot at the south end of Kyle Field. My friend Bud Nelson was hosting a tailgate and yelled for me to come over.

He introduced me to some 10 or more folks, one of whom was an Aggie from Austin. The Austin Aggie told me about a Longhorn coworker in his office who didn't like me. I asked why, and he said I was too much of an Aggie on the radio for his taste. Matter of fact, he disliked me so much that he might have bad thoughts if he saw me crossing a street and he was driving.

I asked for the man's name and business address. He gave it to me and asked what I was going to do. At that moment, I really didn't know.

The next week I put together a box containing an Aggie hat, T-shirt, mug, pennant, and football and basketball media guide. On the pennant, I signed it with a note saying, "Thanks for being such a great fan!" In the mail it went to Austin, not knowing what kind of response the box might bring.

Two to three weeks later, I was walking across that same lot, and Bud and his group were there. The Austin Aggie spotted me and came running over.

He asked if I had sent his coworker a gift box, and I said yes. He told me that Longhorn is now one of my biggest fans. Kill them with kindness. Besides I wanted to feel safe when I walked the streets in Austin!

## Barton Creek Country Club

A story I've told many times down through the years is something that happened in Austin at Barton Creek Country Club. It was an all-A&M event that day, and Aggies had taken over the golf course. On this particular hole, the distance between where my group parked our carts and the tee box was quite a walk. When we got up there, I didn't feel like I had the right club, so I walked back to the cart to change it.

When I got there, the young lady driving the beverage cart pulled up and asked if I wanted a drink. I told her I didn't but that the guys at the tee box might want something if she didn't mind waiting until after they hit. While we waited, I asked her if she was a student.

"I've already graduated," she replied in a frosty tone.

I asked, "Oh, really? From where?"

"*The* University," the young lady said in the same frosty tone.

"Well, you're going to have to help me because I'm not sure where *the* university is," I said.

"The University of Texas, and we feel sorry for you people," she said with icicles hanging on her words.

I stood there for a few seconds and then shared my next thought: "Hmmm, well, I hate to tell you this, but I just don't know of any Texas A&M graduates who are beverage cart drivers on a golf course."

She slammed the lid on the ice chest and said she'd come back. But she didn't, and no amount of vigorous waving and whistling from my fellow golfers changed her mind.

Near the end of the round, I confessed what had happened, and they enjoyed a good laugh at the story.

## No Return Address

After six games during the 2009 Aggie football season, the team was 3–3 after a loss in Manhattan, Kansas, to Kansas State. Up next was the Texas Tech Red Raiders and their high-flying offense in Lubbock. The loss to Kansas State was a blowout, 62–14, and the Red Raider fans were licking their chops.

Many folks back home were telling me that not only were they not going to make the seven-hour drive, but they would not listen to the radio and would not watch the game on television. Sounded like Dave Elmendorf and I would be talking to ourselves.

The expected blowout did not happen. The Aggies defeated the Red Raiders 52–30. Later, I heard how many A&M fans' plans were interrupted as news of the Aggies play started leaking out. Gatherings were being interrupted as fans were sneaking a listen to the radio or checking the television—everyone would join in, and it turned into a listening party or watching party. Dave and I were having a great time on the radio! It was a happy flight home.

The next week, the mail-room staff at Kyle Field brought me a small package that had no return address but a Midlothian, Texas, postmark. It was addressed to "Texas A&M Broadcaster, Kyle Field, College Station, Texas."

I didn't know whether to open it or not. It sat on my desk until late afternoon. It was very light and only big enough to hold something a little larger than a softball.

Four o'clock rolled around, and I decided to open it very slowly and cautiously. The item inside was wrapped with a note laying on top.

The note said, "I thought you might need these after the game against Tech on Saturday. You two fellows [meaning Elmendorf and me] likely dirtied your shorts during the game."

Removing the wrapping paper, I found two pairs of brand-new underwear.

If the intent was to upset us, it didn't work. I featured the story in the pregame prior to our next broadcast. I wanted to get them framed, but my wife, Leanne, said that would be a little too much. I kept them in the box they came in as a part of my memorabilia collection.

## Shout-Outs

One of the fun things about the radio broadcasts were the texts and emails we would receive during a game. Since these often came in from all over the world, we made every effort to give names and locations.

Messages that meant a lot were from our Aggies in the military. Sometimes they came during times of conflict. The message could come from just about anywhere—war zones, Europe, and the Far East as well as from all over the United States. Often they would message back and say thank you and that it made them feel like they were back on campus and at the game.

Four former students sent an email and a photo of them sitting around a laptop and listening to an Aggie game late at night. They were working construction on the new US embassy in Moscow.

Two couples sat in a rooftop café in Rome, watching the game on a laptop and sending encouragement to the team.

At some point during the football season, we would hear from deer hunters, campers, bird hunters, fishermen, farmers, or folks in far west Texas walking around outside trying to pick up the game on the radio.

Then there were the requests for shout-outs to a loved one in the hospital. Some were close to making the final trip to heaven, and sometimes the family would text or email saying the shout-out had put a smile on that Aggie's face.

For all the complaining we do about the intrusive nature of cell phones, these texts and emails added a special element to the broadcasts. The messages we received reminded us how special it was and is to be an Aggie and to follow Texas A&M.

## The Committee

There is a group of us that meets once a week for coffee. We solve all the world's problems during sessions that run two hours or more.

Currently, you must be 70 years old or older and have thick skin. You never know what will be said to you or about you, but it's all in fun.

In late June 2018, I went to Wichita Falls to see some high school classmates. I also had breakfast with Max Vordenbaum, an Aggie, and his son August, who was getting close to graduating from A&M. Max, August, and I met at the Highway Café on the Old Jacksboro Highway at 7:30 a.m. I arrived early at 6:45.

At about 7:00 a.m., the Wichita Falls committee arrived. There were about the same number as our College Station group, but all were older. They sat close by, so I could hear everything being said.

They discussed almost the same topics we covered: sports, politics, where was so-and-so, doctor's appointments, golf, and so on. After a while, I walked over and introduced myself and told them about the College Station committee.

The fellow sitting closest to me said his daughter went to Texas A&M. She visited the campus at the last minute but came back and told her father she was going to be an Aggie.

She told him, "Daddy, you would love it. The boys have short hair and wear jeans and cowboy boots!"

## The Hike in Colorado

My friend and Texas A&M former student Clinton Seal said I should include this story in the book.

For football and baseball games, I sat in a booth with other people and talked into a microphone. In basketball, half of the people sat behind me and the other half sat across from me on the floor.

Because I wore a headset and was always watching the action of the game on a field and hardwood floor, I never really thought about how many people were listening. It always surprised me when someone recognized my voice and asked if I was Dave South. I have always felt honored and humbled by that.

Once, though, I was playing golf with former player, coach, and athletic administrator John Thornton, and he invited a third person to play with us. After we finished, John would later tell me his buddy said he would not play golf with me again. My voice intimidated him, and he couldn't concentrate on his game.

Probably the most unusual place someone recognized my voice was in the middle of nowhere outside of Pagosa Springs, Colorado. Leanne and I went on a hike that took us along a river then down into a valley. When we reached the valley, Leanne was about 20 yards ahead of me. Coming our way were three women: a grandmother, her adult daughter, and her granddaughter.

Leanne said hello, and when they got to me, I said, "Good morning!" The daughter stopped, turned around, and said, "You're Dave South." Those were the only three people we saw the entire time we were on the trail, and one just happened to be an Aggie and a football fan!

## Summer Float Trip on the Comal

There was a period during the summer in the late 1980s and early 1990s when we met several other couples in New Braunfels for the weekend.

We would float on either the Guadalupe River or the Comal, depending on the water flow that summer. Both are a lot of fun, and there were always a lot of people.

The first day, we floated down the Guadalupe River. The next day, we floated down the Comal, which usually is a peaceful trip in cool, spring-fed water.

There was a take-out point with a dock where you pass your tubes up, pull yourself up onto the dock, and then walk up a long flight of stairs to a parking lot where you left a car to take you back to the starting point.

On this day, the Comal was packed, and we ran into a log jam at the take-out. Among the many there was a group of soldiers from Fort Hood and a group of visitors from Germany. Both groups had been drinking.

Some folks started pushing and shoving as they tried to pull themselves out of the water. Words were exchanged; it started to get ugly.

I didn't have a tube, just a life jacket, so it was easier for me to get to the dock than it was for others. There were several families with children, and some of the kids were frightened from the yelling and started crying.

When I got up on the dock, I spoke matter-of-factly to both the soldiers and the German visitors. I then helped two of the moms onto the dock and folks in the water started passing the kids to us. The moms on the dock watched those kids until their mothers could get out of the water.

When all the women and children were out, three other men and I started helping others still in the water get onto the deck.

So after all the hullabaloo with drunk soldiers and German visitors and crying children, I gave a hand to one man and was pulling him out of the water when he asked, "Hey, Dave, when is the first R. C. Slocum television show?"

Aggie fans love their football.

## Fort Davis, Texas

Our favorite vacation destination is Fort Davis, Texas, and the Davis Mountains State Park located three miles outside of town.

In 2010, we had a September open date on the football schedule, so we loaded up the motorhome and drove out to Fort Davis for the weekend. Once we got settled in, we found out that Friday night was homecoming at Fort Davis High School.

What else is better on a fall Friday night in Texas than a high school football game, right? As we were walking to the bleachers after buying Frito pies and sodas, I ran into Ray Hendryx, owner of radio station KVLF in Alpine. Ray is an Aggie. On this night, he was broadcasting the Fort Davis Indians–Midland Trinity Christian six-man football game.

KVLF also broadcasted Texas A&M football games, so whenever we were in Fort Davis, I would drive to Alpine to see Ray. He asked if I would like to join him on the radio. I thanked him for the offer but declined, saying I just wanted to watch the game.

Halftime that night featured the crowning of the homecoming queen. About five or six beautiful young ladies were escorted onto the field by their fathers.

The PA announcer read a short bio on each girl. The one I remember was for the nominee whose favorite activity was climbing water towers. That was a real west Texas girl!

Fort Davis won the game, 42–40. The next morning, I went to the grocery store in Fort Davis. Out front were some young men, and they were having a bake sale.

I walked over and started talking to them and found out that they were members of the football team. Later in the schedule, they would play a game against a school located near the Dallas-Fort Worth metroplex. The money raised would help the team get tickets to a college football game in the metroplex on Saturday.

As we're talking, the head coach drives up. He gets out, walks over to me, and says, "I think you must be Dave South."

The night before, Ray had announced on the radio that Leanne and I were at the game. The game was also being broadcast on the internet. The head coach's son was going to Texas A&M and listening to the game from College Station. He called his father after the game to tell him we were there!

By the way, there were some fellows from Kerrville at the football game who had ridden to Fort Davis on a motorcycle trip. We started talking, and I said something about Texas A&M. They started talking about Johnny Manziel and gave me a preview of what to expect when he took the field. Everything they said came true.

## La. Tech

A drunk Cajun fan wanted to beat me up during the 1996 football season. The Aggies had dropped three of their first four games. Up next was a home game against Louisiana Tech on October 9 that Texas A&M won, 63–13.

For as long as I can remember, when someone talked about Louisiana Tech, they also referred to them as "La. Tech." I did that during the first half.

At halftime, I walked up a level to the press box, and as I walked by the operations booth, Penny King opened the door. Penny was an associate athletic director and answered the phone in the operations booth during the games.

She asked me if I had referred to Louisiana Tech as La. Tech, and I said yes, most everyone does.

She said, "I just got a call from someone with a heavy Cajun accent who said he was calling from Rockport, Texas. He is not happy that you are calling them La. Tech."

I reiterated that it was a common practice, but I would ease up in the second half.

Quick note: In 1996, everyone still had a landline, we still used telephone books, and my name and address were listed.

Later, after we had turned off the light, sometime after 10:00 p.m, our home phone rang.

A woman's voice asked if this was the Dave South who broadcasts the Aggie games. I said yes.

"Were you calling Louisiana Tech 'La. Tech' on the radio today?" she asked. Again, I replied yes.

"Well, I have a crazy Cajun cousin who has driven up from Rockport, and he is looking for you," she said. "He's drunk and says he is going to beat you up."

She explained that she told him I normally stayed at a hotel on Texas Avenue after the games and that I drive a purple car. She warned me that he might grab a phone book and look me up when he didn't find the car. To top it off, she said he was a mean drunk, so I shouldn't answer the door at all that night.

I had been sleepy but now was wide awake, wondering what the neighbors would think if they saw me rolling around in the middle of the street with some drunk guy.

We did the smart thing and called the College Station Police. A police car patrolled our neighborhood for the rest of the night.

We didn't play at home again until October 19 against Kansas State. The university police department had been notified about the Rockport fan. Just to be on the safe side, a uniformed officer stood outside the radio booth the entire game.

Fortunately, the La. Tech fan never showed.

## Oldest Living Aggie

I always enjoyed my trips to San Angelo. My wife, Leanne, grew up about two hours from San Angelo in McCamey, Texas.

I spoke to the San Angelo Aggies several times during my career and made several lifelong friends—Stormy Kimrey, to mention one. Stormy, for many years, would pick up and stay in College Station during the football season. He was always at the coach's radio show every week with a group of his friends. Stormy was also the one who always asked me to speak in San Angelo.

On one trip, I met the oldest (at that time) living Aggie. He was full of energy and a regular attendee at those meetings. At this meeting, they had a birthday cake to celebrate his turning 101. His name was Ossie W. Greene, and he was in the class of 1915. He likely was born about 1893 or 1894.

As I'm speaking, he is sitting right in front of me and raises his hand. I stop and recognize him.

"Do you wear a toupee?" he asked. I said no and gave a little tug on my hair, and he said thank you. I have no clue what prompted that.

I wish I had interviewed him. I can only imagine the stories he could've told. I wonder what he would think if he visited Texas A&M in 2019.

## The Other Oldest Living Aggie

The other oldest living Aggie that I met was in Abilene at the Abilene A&M Club. This gentleman was 104 years old. He was bright, alert, and spry. But I didn't know that at first. They introduced him to me, and I related that I had met a gentleman (who had passed away by this time) in San Angelo a few years back who was 101. But at 104, the gentleman in Abilene was the oldest living Aggie I had ever met.

Later, after finishing my presentation, I asked the man if we could have our picture taken together, and he said yes. So I walked across the room and asked if one of the A&M club members would take our picture. When I turned around to walk back, the 104-year-old gentleman was right behind me.

I apologized and told him that I didn't mean for him to have to walk all the way across the room. He replied that he wasn't a cripple!

## Tiger Fans Express Their Feelings

We were in Baton Rouge to play the LSU Tigers before we entered the SEC. I went out to the car to put some bags in the back as we were getting ready to go to Tiger Stadium.

I was standing at the front edge of the parking lot. Past that was about 40 yards of grass and then the feeder road, and on the other side of the feeder road was I-10.

Two guys in a pick-up truck stopped on the feeder road and got out. The driver stayed on his side, and the passenger was standing on the edge of the grass that separated us.

The passenger yelled out, "###&&##$@@*** you %&##### Aggie!" I was wearing a maroon shirt, so I was an easy target.

There was a lot of traffic out on I-10, but I could hear everything he said.

I cupped my right hand behind my right ear and yelled, "What"? Again, he yelled, "###&&##$@@*** you %&##### Aggie."

So again, I repeated, "What?" and for a third time he yelled out, "###&&##$@@*** you %&##### Aggie!"

There was a half-inch wire cable running along the edge of the parking lot, so I walked toward the cable and said, "Hold on, I am coming over there."

I guess they didn't want to be friends because they jumped into the truck and sped away. I just wanted to explain that what they were saying wasn't factual.

## Tony Barone and San Angelo Road Trip

One of the things that I got to do a lot of was travel with various coaches to different events. The San Angelo A&M Club called and asked if Tony Barone, Texas A&M's basketball coach at that time, would come and speak to their club. I went down and visited with Tony, and he agreed to go if I would go with him. I told him we'd have to drive out there, and he was fine with doing that.

It was a Wednesday meeting and would take us about seven hours to drive, so we left Tuesday afternoon and spent the night in Mason. As we drove to San Angelo the next day, I emphasized to Tony what a great group of people we would find at this Aggie Club, how he was going to like these folks, and that this meeting would be a lot of fun.

As we walk into the meeting room, the first guy who walks up to Tony sticks his hand out and introduces himself. Then he asks, "You know, Coach, why is it all basketball coaches are short, fat Italians?" I'm thinking to myself, "Aw, brother." Tony kind of glances at me with a slight glare and then responds, "Because we're good at answering stupid questions!"

## Bob and the Golf Tees

My friend Bob Ammon from Waco is a staunch Baylor fan, so when I started working at Texas A&M there was some good-natured ribbing between us.

During the 1990s, I had a box with hundreds of Texas A&M golf tees that I passed out to the golfers in the athletic department. Bob ran a driving range in Waco back then. I kept 100 or more of those tees in the back of my car and on a visit to his driving range dumped them into a large tub with complimentary golf tees by the door.

It took a couple of weeks before he discovered them and then two or three days to pick them all out! He loves his Bears.

## Rosebud-Lott Traffic Stop

Karl Kapchinski and I had gone to Waco for the Texas A&M–Baylor baseball series. On the way back, I was stopped in Rosebud-Lott for speeding.

I got out with my driver's license and proof of insurance. At that time, I was driving a vehicle provided by Texas A&M Athletics, so the insurance listed TAMU Athletics as the responsible party.

The officer read that and asked why. I told him that I worked for the athletic department. He asked if I was a coach, and I said no. He asked if I was anyone famous, and I said no.

He looked at me for a moment and then said, "Well, you might be famous someday, and I might run into you. I might even ask you for an autograph and you wouldn't give it to me because I wrote you a ticket. So I'm not going to do it."

I got back in the car and Karl said, "You have got to be one of the luckiest guys in America."

## Correspondence

I've been around long enough that letters turned into emails. I have saved many of those, and they will eventually go to the Texas A&M Archives at Cushing Library.

One letter came in back in the mid-1990s from a student about to graduate. He wrote that while at A&M, he listened to many of the games. He was moving back home and would continue to listen.

He said that I had been his eyes even when he went to a game. This student had been blind since birth, and the broadcasts meant a lot to him as he followed Texas A&M sports.

His letter reminded me of the following question and answer: "Who can graduate from Texas A&M? Anyone who wants to." That letter touched my heart and is certainly one I will not forget.

On November 29, 2017, the following email came in. Matthew gave me permission to use it in this book.

Dave,

I am sitting here at work today listening to some of your calls that I listened to live at my house when I was a kid. I listened to you as I tossed the football in the yard with my brothers. We all wanted to play at A&M. We listened live in 2004 when Colorado came to town, and we went to overtime to win on a fumble. We listened in 2006 when A&M went to Stillwater and won a thriller. We even listened live in 2007 when we beat Texas, and I was camping with my father. We were fishing on a cool November day while listening to that one. He was at A&M when you started, by the way. He was a student during the '86 A&M– Baylor game. That wasn't the only fond memory—there were so many others. I could go on for days.

I ended up attending A&M between 2008 and 2012, and even though I went to every game, I would go running in the evenings and listen to your broadcast. It put me back in the moment. When the stress of finals or other hardships came along, your voice was a nice reprieve. You brought more joy to more people than I think you know.

I hope you get this message because I've wanted to thank you for some time. Your voice makes me think of time spent with cousins, and grandparents. It makes me think of my bothers, and it makes me think of my mom and dad. I should give my folks a call, by the way. You see, my father and I had a difficult relationship as I got older, but Aggie football and Dave South on the radio always brought us together. It still does. At the end of your broadcasts, when I hear you call to pray for our first responders and wounded warriors, I am reminded of what is important. And it's a lot more than football. But Aggie football, basketball, and baseball have been fun, win or lose, because you helped make it that way. Thank you so much. If I ever get to meet you, it would be an honor.

Matthew E. Wallace
Class of 2012

Thank you, to Matthew and to others who, down through the years, let me be a part of their lives.

## 6

# Games

### The Good, the Bad, and
### Some of My Most Memorable Games

### Far Reaches of Space

This story happened on Thanksgiving night, November 28, 1985, before the Texas A&M versus Texas game at Kyle Field.

Roger Lewis was the producer on the broadcast in those days. He would keep us on track for commercials, station IDs, reader cards, and messages from the studio in Dallas.

We were very close to airtime when the phone connecting us to Dallas rang. It was unusual for a call that close to the start of the broadcast. Lewis answered and said OK, he would tell Dave.

I took off my headset, and Roger said, "The Shuttle astronauts are going to listen to our broadcast tonight."

Roger glanced at his stopwatch and pointed at me. We were live and on the air. He kept pointing at me. I kept looking back at him. He pointed again and said put on your headset. I did, but I couldn't think of anything to say.

It was likely only about 30 to 40 seconds of dead air, but it seemed like five minutes. There was something about sending the game to outer space that gave me a brain freeze. I spaced out.

In those days we did not record the games, so I have no idea how I opened the broadcast. What I do know is that the Aggies beat the Longhorns 42–10 to win the SWC championship!

## 2017 Nicholls State Game

In my last season of Aggie football, I have been asked to go back from time to time and reflect on moments that stand out in my career. Last week, I talked about my first game in 1985 as the designated play-by-play announcer for Texas A&M.

Today, my first home broadcast at Kyle Field.

The Aggies had started the week before with a road game in Birmingham and a loss to Alabama. On September 21, Northeast Louisiana came to College Station and gave the Aggies a run for their money. It was tied at halftime at 14 each, but the boys in maroon would outscore Northeast 17–3 in the second half with 10 points coming in the fourth quarter.

A&M would grind it out on the ground. Anthony Toney, Keith Woodside, and Roger Vick combined for a total of 277 yards rushing. Tony Franklin would kick three field goals, the longest of which was 35 yards

The Aggies would not lose at home that year on their way to their first SWC championship in 18 years.

# 2017 Florida Game

Today, as we get ready to play Florida here in Gainesville, I want to go back to the last Big 12 game and the first SEC game played by the Aggies.

Both of those games turned into losses . . . so before we talk about those . . . how about we talk about the last win in the Big 12? That came against Kansas in Lawrence 61–7 in 2011. The Aggies' first SEC win came against Arkansas, 58–10, in October 2012.

The first Big 12 game I broadcasted was at Kyle Field on September 28, 1996. The Aggie hosted Colorado and would drop the conference opener, 24–10. Texas A&M fumbled the opening kickoff at the Aggie 28-yard line. Then the Buffaloes called what I still consider one of the best plays run against A&M in my 32 seasons. Rae Carruth, a wide receiver, ran a reverse and scored on a 28-yard run . . . one play, 28 yards, and Colorado never trailed in the game. That was the start of Big 12 play for the Aggies that would end when A&M moved to the SEC after the 2011 season.

Moving forward to 2012. The Aggies were due to start the season with a game against Louisiana Tech, but the threat of a hurricane on the Gulf Coast canceled that tilt. With both teams having the same open date later in the season, it was moved to October 13.

That meant the Aggies would not have a tune-up game before playing Florida on September 8 at Kyle Field. Florida had one game under their belt, and their coaching staff knew more about their squad than perhaps the Aggie coaches knew about their team. Even with that setting the stage, the Aggies had a good first half and led at halftime, 17–10. The Gators would shut the Aggies out in the second half and score 10 points to win, 20–17.

To this day, I still wonder what the result would have been had A&M been able to play the Louisiana Tech game as scheduled.

MEMORY MOMENT
## 2017 Louisiana Game

There have been some stories written leading into this game against Louisiana Lafayette referencing the game on September 14, 1996.

You would need to go back to the week before to get the start of the story. In game one that year, number 12–ranked Texas A&M played Brigham Young (BYU) for the first time since the 1990 Holiday Bowl in the Pigskin Kick-Off Classic in Provo, Utah.

Texas A&M lost a hard-fought game, 41–37, in Provo, giving up 15 fourth-quarter points to the Cougars. A&M turned the ball over two times with only one leading to points—a touchdown.

Perhaps the Aggies were a little down mentally when they rolled into Lafayette because the Ragin Cajuns defeated the Aggies, 29–22.

Texas A&M fumbled four times and lost all four. Branndon Stewart was intercepted four times. Two of the interceptions were returned for touchdowns. One of the fumbles went for a touchdown. A&M was 0–2 after two games, would finish up 6–6, and fail to make a bowl game.

# Oklahoma 77-Texas A&M 0

**The Texas A&M–Oklahoma game in Norman, Oklahoma, on November 3, 2003, was the longest day in my tenure with the Aggies.**

Texas A&M entered the game with a 3–5 mark in Dennis Franchione's first season as the Aggie head coach.

The game summary said the following:

Jason White tied a school record with five touchdown passes and Oklahoma's defense didn't allow a touchdown for a second straight week in the top-ranked Sooners' 77–0 rout of Texas A&M. Oklahoma scored touchdowns on 10 of its first 11 possessions and got its final score of the day when cornerback Derrick Strait scooped up a fumble and returned it 17 yards to the end zone late in the third quarter.

I bring this painful game up for two reasons. We were trying our best to find something good to say. Tim Cassidy was the color analyst that year on the broadcast. It suddenly hit me that he had quit talking. That, by the way, is normal in a game where your team is getting drummed. During a time-out, I looked intently at Tim. He was staring at the field, and I guess he could feel my eyes on him. He slowly turned his head and without hesitation said, "I don't know what to say."

I replied, "I just said wanted to make sure you were still with me."

Back then, we did not have the luxury of stat monitors. My wife, Leanne, used a paper form and kept up with everything from first downs to penalties. The score hit 77–0 before the end of the third quarter. During the quarter break, she asked me to take off the headset.

She asked, "Are you going to use any of this?" I said no.

She stood up and announced that she was going back to the motorhome and would see me after the game. Leanne was one person who welcomed the computer stat programs when they were installed in the press box.

By the way, she was good at giving me an elbow in the side if she felt I was going overboard in talking about the officials.

## Big 12 Championship Game's "Almost" QB Controversy

One game many Aggies and Aggie fans remember is the 1998 Big 12 championship game against Kansas State in the Trans World Dome (as it was called back then) in St. Louis. The Aggies won the game in triple overtime to capture the title. It was a game no one expected Texas A&M to win.

Kansas State was ranked number 1 in the coaches' poll, and many believed a win would set up a mythical national championship match-up in the Fiesta Bowl.

Texas A&M went into that game without its starting quarterback Randy McCown, who'd injured his shoulder the previous week. Running back Sirr Parker was questionable with an injured hamstring.

Things looked bleak until one of the most amazing fourth quarters I have ever seen. The game ended tied, and both teams battled through two overtimes. In the third overtime, quarterback Branndon Stewart hit Sirr Parker, who ran it in for a touchdown to win the game.

Everybody on the Aggie side went crazy. In the radio booth, Mamie Elmendorf, who had been helping on the broadcast, was running back and forth on the table, yelling and screaming. My spotter, Jim Benson, who was a yell leader in the 1960s, had slid down the wall and was crying for joy, which got me teary-eyed. I looked down on the field and saw Dr. Ray Bowen, then the president of Texas A&M. He was laying on his back and moving his arms and legs as if he were making a snow angel!

Later, outside the stadium, I saw the late Ray Dorr, the quarterback coach. During the game, Stewart got hit on a third-down play and had to be helped off the field. With McCown hurt, the backup quarterback was punter Shane Lechler. After punting the ball on fourth down, Lechler came off the field and sat down on the bench to change shoes. Dorr was sitting next to him.

When I saw Ray standing by the team bus after the game, I asked him what he was thinking during the shoe exchange.

Dorr replied, "I looked up at the scoreboard and prayed, 'Lord, don't let it be 100–0!'"

In 2016, I interviewed Lechler prior to the Texas A&M–Arizona State game played in NRG Stadium in Houston. Lechler, who has punted in the NFL since graduating from Texas A&M, had recently joined the Houston Texans. I told him the story about Dorr's comment from the Big 12 championship game. Lechler said he remembers asking Dorr not to call any passing plays because he didn't know any!

Fortunately, Lechler never had to take a snap at quarterback. Stewart recovered and played the rest of the game.

My call of the Sirr Parker touchdown has garnered some attention over the years. It was without a doubt one of the most exciting moments of my career. Later, it was included in a book called *Heart Stoppers and Hail Marys: 100 of the Greatest College Football Finishes (1970–1999).*

What an honor. What a game!

## Overtime Games

During my career at Texas A&M, the overtime rule went into effect for college football and is still being used. The rule was put into place for the bowl games at the end of the 1995 season but was not used in the regular season games until the following year of 1996.

Here are recollections of some memorable overtime games.

Texas A&M defeated Arkansas, 50–43, in an overtime game at AT&T Stadium in Arlington on September 23, 2017. It was the 18th overtime game in A&M history. As of 2017, Arkansas was the only team that Texas A&M had played in three overtime games, winning all three: 35–28 in 2014, 28–21 in 2015, and 50–43 in 2017.

●

Texas A&M's first overtime game came against Oklahoma State at Kyle Field in 1997. Kyle Field still had the open end to the south, and there was a gate in which fans could exit to the parking lots.

The Aggies were down to the Cowboys 19–7 going into the fourth quarter, and the fans were streaming out of the stadium through the south exit. In the fourth quarter, A&M would score 15 points and tie the game at 22.

I remember looking at that south gate and seeing an avalanche of fans trying to make their way back into the stadium to be there for what turned out to be Texas A&M's first win, 28–25.

●

The Aggies would play overtime games multiple times in 2002 (Mizzou and Texas Tech), 2004, 2011 (Mizzou and Kansas State), and 2016 (UCLA and Tennessee). The 2004 season marked the first and only time the Aggies would play three in one season, beating Texas Tech and Colorado but losing to Baylor.

The longest consecutive seasons playing an overtime game counting the 2017 Arkansas game is four in a row. In those four seasons—2014, 2015, 2016, and 2017—Texas A&M won five in a row and sported a 12–6 record in overtime games.

●

The longest game was when the Aggies lost in overtime to Kansas State in 2011, as it went over four overtime periods. It was played in Manhattan, and the Wildcats held on to win, 53–50.

I called every Aggie overtime game through the 2017 season, and let me tell you, they were heart-pounding every time. I will say the 2018 LSU overtime game was the best ever.

## Some of My Favorite Games

This is not an easy thing to do, but here were some of my favorite games to broadcast.

1985: Texas A&M 31, NE Louisiana 17. This was my first Aggie win as the "voice of Texas A&M football." Enough said.

1985 Cotton Bowl: Texas A&M 36, Auburn 16. The Aggie goal line stand in the fourth quarter and stopping Bo Jackson in the first half were as good as it gets in a football game.

1986: Texas A&M 31, Baylor 30. This game was voted the best game of the decade. My heart fluttered when Tony Thompson juggled the ball on his game-winning catch. My mentor Frank Fallon did the color with me.

1987 Cotton Bowl: Texas A&M 35, Notre Dame 10. Outside of the Aggie family, no one gave the Aggies any chance of winning this game.

1991 Holiday Bowl: Texas A&M 65, Brigham Young 14. The Aggie defense knocked out Heisman winner Ty Detmer. Bucky Richardson led a determined, and creative, offensive attack. What was fun for me was getting separated from the Aggie official party at a luncheon on the aircraft carrier *Lexington*. I was not wearing any Aggie gear, so I fit right in with the BYU fans. Sitting at a table with eight of them, they were moaning about playing a lower-ranked team and how when they would win, there would be no real recognition. It came time to recognize the travel party for A&M, and we were asked to stand up, which I did. That started the string of apologies.

1993: Texas A&M 18, Texas 9. The Aggies were undefeated in the SWC and headed for a championship. A&M was ranked number eight and was playing the Longhorns at home on Thanksgiving night.

1995 Alamo Bowl: Texas A&M 22, Michigan 20. My buddy Kyle Bryant got a "kick out of life" with a big field goal night. Michigan had a running back with one of the toughest names ever to pronounce: Tim Biakabutuka.

1997: Texas A&M 28, Oklahoma State 25. First overtime game ever.

1998: Texas A&M 28, #2 Nebraska 21. Jamar Toombs made one of the most determined runs ever carrying defenders on his back. On one run, he was looking at the south-end big screen and could see the defense chasing him and knew which way to go.

1999: The Bonfire Game. Texas A&M 20, Texas 16. The good Lord knew that Aggies everywhere needed this win. The University of Texas band delivered a classy, respectful halftime performance. It was the most difficult game I ever had to broadcast. Brian Gamble falling to his knees after recovering the fumble that sealed the win summed up what we all were feeling that day.

2002: Texas A&M 30, #1 Oklahoma 26. R. C. Slocum threw the Sooners a curve by starting Reggie McNeal.

2012: Texas A&M 58, Arkansas 10. The beginning of a wild season led by eventual Heisman Trophy winner Johnny Manziel.

2012: Texas A&M 29, Alabama 24. The Aggies caught lightning in a bottle in Tuscaloosa. One of the most memorable plays of Johnny Manziel's career.

2013 Cotton Bowl: Texas A&M 41, Oklahoma 13. Manziel shines in a post-Heisman performance.

2013 Chick-fil-A Bowl: Texas A&M 52, Duke 48. Two crazy, completely different halves of football. Johnny Manziel ends his college career with a win.

2016: Texas A&M men's basketball versus Northern Iowa (UNI), Chesapeake Arena, Oklahoma City. Billy Kennedy and the Aggie men's basketball team traveled to Oklahoma City for the first and second rounds of the NCAA men's basketball tournament, March 18 and 20, 2016. A&M opened against Wisconsin Green Bay and won going away, 92–65. In the other game, the University of Northern Iowa beat Texas in a barn burner, 75–72. The second-round game on March 20, matched the Aggies against the Panthers. The Aggies would start a veteran lineup: Jalen Jones, Tyler Davis, Anthony Collins, Alex Caruso, and Danuel House. The Panthers would counter with Bennett Koch, Paul Jesperson, Matt Bohannon, Wes Washpun, and Jeremy Morgan. The Aggies were 27–8 entering the game, and the Panthers were 23–13. UNI had a great first half and built a 10-point lead, 32–22.

For the game, the Panthers were 12 of 34 from the three-point line, and the Aggies, a not-so-good 7 of 31. With about 1:40 left in the second half, the Aggies started fouling to stop the clock. UNI hit their free throws, and with less than a minute left, the Panthers had a 12-point lead. John Thornton and I were working the game, and I had already conceded the win to the Panthers, wishing them well against Oklahoma in the sweet 16 the next weekend. Little did we know that was not to be the case. The NCAA would later report that this was the biggest final-minute comeback of all time. It beat the previous record held by San Diego State when they came back from 11 down with 59 seconds to go. The Aggies managed three more points in 26 fewer seconds. Over the course of 33 of the most electrifying seconds of basketball I have ever seen, Texas A&M forced four turnovers and scored six baskets and one free throw to tie the game at 71. Vanderbilt coach Kevin Stallings reviewed the last 40-plus seconds and reported that 11 things had to happen for Texas A&M to win the game. If just one of the 11 failed to take place, the Aggies would have lost in regulation.

After being down by 10 at halftime, Texas A&M would outscore UNI by 10 in the second half, 49–39. That would force not one but two overtimes (OTs). Each team scored 12 in the first OT with the Aggies winning the second OT 9–5. Final score 91–88. Alex Caruso scored 25, and Danuel House posted 22. Five Aggies scored in double figures. Jalen Jones and Caruso each had nine rebounds, and House had eight. The Aggies also had a decided advantage in the paint, outscoring the Panthers 44–20. When Leanne and I were on our way back to College Station early the next morning, my phone blew up with people sending emails and texts. It seems that they, like me, had given up with a minute to go and turned it off. They all asked the same question: "What happened?" I watched the whole thing from courtside, and even I am not sure what happened. But I am sure that it was the greatest basketball game I ever called.

## Halftime Shows

Part of the fun of attending college games is watching what happens before the game and at halftime. We are usually on the air during pregame festivities but have a break during halftime. Here are some performances that have stood out to me over the years.

●

There is no doubt that the best halftime in college football is the Fightin' Texas Aggie band. From my first game to my last game, whenever the band stepped off, I got cold chills. They simply are the best.

Fans from other schools agreed. It was rare that we didn't walk into an opponent's stadium and have someone ask us if the Aggie band was coming. The only people who didn't like the band coming were those in charge of concessions. The fans wouldn't leave their seats! Instead, they stayed to watch the Aggies perform at halftime.

●

Many college bands have impressive traditions as a part of their performances, like when the Aggie band runs off the field after making the block "T."

Another impressive halftime tradition is the Ohio State band when they "dot the I." One student is selected to dot the I and is led onto the field by the drum major. Once I saw an interview with one of the students selected, and you could tell by the look on his face that it was a real honor.

Other than the Aggie band, I have to say that the Prairie View A&M band delivers one of the more energetic and entertaining halftime performances. It seemed like Texas A&M always tried to find a way to bring them to Kyle Field during football season. I know Aggie fans always looked forward to their coming.

●

For me, the most moving, impressive pregame ritual happens at Auburn, when the war eagle flies around the stadium. If you've never attended a Texas A&M–Auburn football game at Auburn, I would encourage you to do so. Before you go, look up the history of the war eagle. During the ceremony one year, it looked for a moment like the eagle was going to fly right into our radio booth!

●

The best basketball halftime I ever saw happened at Murray State back in the 1970s. A men's ROTC group tap-danced their entire routine and got a standing ovation and a curtain call!

As far as halftimes at Aggie basketball games, the best ones are the little dribbler teams playing an abbreviated game. When those little guys and girls heave the ball into the basket, the crowd goes wild! It's just great fun to watch these younger athletes give it their all on the court.

# 7

# Goofs

Here are some stories that qualify as not some of my finer moments, but when you reach your 70s, you stop taking yourself too seriously!

## Will Bolt

In Bryan–College Station, when you have a family pet that is not doing well, your vet may recommend Texas A&M's veterinary hospital for further care. We had one of our dogs there, and a vet student had taken us to see her in a rest area for the pets with wire doors at the front.

We have an assistant baseball coach, Will Bolt, who handles the offense for Coach Rob Childress. Will grew up in Texas but played baseball at Nebraska. Will was a very good player and had some good games against Texas A&M.

Next to our dog was another dog, and above the wire door was a sign with a printed name, "Will Bolt." I told the student with us that I knew the owner of that dog. He was one of our assistant baseball coaches.

I ask why his name was on the sign and in such big letters. She asked what I meant. I said his name, "Will Bolt." She replied, saying that that was not a person's name. It was a notice to the staff that if you open the door, the dog "will bolt."

Oh. I half expected someone to step out and say, "Here's your sign."

## Las Vegas Valet Parking

There was a trip to Las Vegas in 2001 for a basketball tournament. The tournament was originally scheduled to be played in the ballroom of a casino hotel, but one of the participating teams refused to play there, so it was moved to a local high school gymnasium.

To save money on the trip, I did not valet park at our hotel. Instead, I parked in a remote lot and dragged my radio equipment, briefcase, and backpack back and forth between the hotel and my rental car.

On the last night there, as I made the hike to the main doors, I walked over to the valet parking stand to ask the cost to valet park. The young man asked if I was staying at the hotel, and I said yes. He replied, "It's free."

In case you're wondering, no, I have no explanation for why I didn't ask earlier.

## Not What I Thought

Texas A&M was matched up in an SWC game in the mid-1980s. I will not mention the opponent or the player for the Aggies.

It appeared to me that an Aggie defensive back had made an outstanding move and intercepted the ball as the other team was driving. I gave the A&M player more than his fair share of radio time and went on about the move he made on the play.

The next week, I saw secondary coach Curly Hallman (1982–1987) and told him what a great move his guy had made on the ball.

He laughed and told me the defensive back had fallen, so the quarterback couldn't see him. The receiver was standing about 3 yards behind our guy. As he stood up, the ball hit him right in the hands, and he somehow managed to hang on to it.

You have to wonder how many times that happens during a season, where it looks like a player made a great play, but it's really the result of a mistake.

## Cotton Bowl Security

Since 9/11, security at all game venues has increased.

Bomb dogs now sniff all the equipment bags, including everything the team is bringing into the stadium. The bags the broadcasters carry in also get searched.

Before the 2005 Cotton Bowl, I got an email asking that we set up the radio booth on Thursday before the Saturday game.

Ed Hadden, our engineer, and I met at Fair Park and then took our equipment up to the booth. It took about an hour to set up everything and then make the connection with the studio for an air check. It all went as expected.

Next, I sought out Cotton Bowl security so that they could inspect the booth and, if needed, bring up the bomb dog. It took me longer to find a security person than it did to set up the booth.

When I found their office, I told them we were ready for them. They had no idea what I was talking about. They found their boss, and I repeated that we were ready for the inspection. He laughed and said that setting up early was not for their benefit, but ours.

He explained, "The Cotton Bowl is getting old. We have rats, and some of the rats have been chewing through various wires in the stadium."

"Is your equipment working?" he asked.

I said yes.

He replied, "I'll see you on Saturday."

## The Water Buffalo and the Wildcats

The Aggies were in Boulder to play the Colorado Buffaloes. The team arrived on Friday and went to the stadium for a walk-through. The squad went out onto the field only to discover that it was time to run Ralphie the Buffalo, which they did every day at the same time.

Ralphie had on a harness with metal loops. Ropes were attached to the loops that students held on to.

They backed Ralphie's trailer up to the corner where I was standing and attached the ropes. Coach Slocum moved the team to the center of the field, and the run started. Students ran Ralphie along the edge of Coors Field to the other side of the field in the opposite corner, where another trailer was waiting. Once inside, the bull knew she was going to be fed, which was her incentive to run.

The team got a kick out this, and it was fun to watch.

Two games later, the Aggies were in Manhattan, Kansas, to play the Kansas State Wildcats. I was standing in the same corner of the field where I had been in Boulder two weeks earlier. A fellow in a Kansas State shirt came up and asked, "Do you think the coach would mind if we brought in the water buffalo?"

"The water buffalo?" I replied.

"Yes," he said.

"You guys are the wildcats," I said, confused.

"Yes," he said.

"What are you doing with a water buffalo?" I asked, still confused.

"What?" he asked.

"What are you doing with a water buffalo?" I asked again.

"Oh, no, it's not an animal. It's a large tank on wheels that has water in the tank," he explained. "We call it a water buffalo."

I thought about explaining my confusion based on the Colorado trip but instead just walked away laughing to myself and at myself.

## The Sun Bowl Interview

On December 28, 1985, I worked the Sun Bowl in El Paso between Arizona and Georgia. The game ended in a 13–13 tie.

This broadcast was a CBS radio production. That meant it was going out across the country. Every major market from New York to LA would carry this broadcast.

The producer, Bill O'Connell, had gone all-out to find the halftime guest I would interview. As we approached halftime, he left the booth but could not find the guest.

He alerted me that he was looking for a new guest and would be back soon. Halftime had started by the time Bill returned with a well-dressed lady and escorted her down to the second level of the booth where I was standing. He handed me a note with something scribbled on it.

I started to ad-lib, buying time while trying to read his handwriting. I turned the note upside down, but it still did not make sense. Finally, in desperation, I just winged it. The conversation went like this:

ME: Hello my name is Dave South, and we are meeting for the first time. What is your name?

GUEST: Katherine Ortega.

ME: Ms. Ortega, what is it you do?

GUEST: I am the treasurer of the United States.

ME: You'll have to help me. I am not sure about this office.

GUEST: I have certain duties that I perform. I am appointed by the president and confirmed by the Senate.

ME: I take it you are a big football fan.

GUEST: Not really. Some friends invited me, so I drove down from Las Cruces.

ME: Well, we've run out of time, so thank you so very much for joining us.

The people listening had to think I was one of the dumbest people on earth.

# 8

# People

Throughout my career, I've been fortunate to meet some interesting and famous people as well as work with some talented and humble people. Here are stories about some of those folks.

## Frank Fallon

This man impacted my career starting in the late 1960s and still has an influence on me to this day.

The late Frank Fallon was one of the finest broadcasters, and finest men, that I ever met and worked with. Many remember Frank for his work as the Baylor Bears broadcaster for 43 years, but he could do it all and do it to perfection.

When I say he could do it all, I mean he could do football, basketball, baseball, track and field, and golf. His talents were unlimited. He did radio and television and worked games at every level, from high school to college to the pros. Outside of radio, he was the "Voice of the Final Four" for two decades.

Over the course of his career, Frank was inducted into the Texas High School Football Hall of Fame and the Baylor Athletics Hall of Fame and was the 2001 recipient of the Chris Schenkel Award from the National Football Foundation and College Football Hall of Fame.

The Texas Sportswriters Association named Frank one of the "Top 10 All-Time Radio Play-by-Play Announcers." Five times he was named

Sportscaster of the Year by the Texas Association of Broadcasters, and he was a seven-time winner of the Associated Press's Best Radio Play-by-Play Announcer Award.

Even though Frank had strong Baylor ties, Texas A&M asked him to host the football coach's television show with Gene Stallings back in the 1970s.

I worked at KWTX in Waco for two years before I had an opportunity to work with him. During that time, I watched how he prepared for games and the professionalism he displayed when working a sporting event. Then, starting in 1970, Frank and I spent the next 10 years working together broadcasting high school football games and Baylor basketball games. For four or five years, we broadcasted the SWC track and field championships.

We also shared play-by-play duties on a few Baylor baseball games. By that I mean we switched out every few innings doing play-by-play only. There was no color analyst on the broadcasts.

I saw his professionalism in action during the few years we broadcasted the 10- to 12-year-old state little league baseball tournament in Waco. We sat behind the backstop in folding chairs with our equipment and materials on a card table. Yet Frank never changed his approach or his preparation.

My career as a college football broadcaster also began in 1970, when Frank set up my audition for the old Southwest Conference Football Radio Network.

Some of our greatest times together were the car trips to Houston, Dallas, Fort Worth, Austin, and College Station. That's when I would ask questions about his approach to games and about his preparation for those games.

Early in my career with the Aggies, the SWC radio network didn't have a set broadcast team for each school, only a play-by-play announcer. During conference play, the home-team announcer did play-by-play while the visiting team's play-by-play announcer worked as the color analyst.

I found it strange to have Frank in the booth doing color with me when the Aggies played Baylor. I think that only happened twice, but it felt strange both times.

I have said many times that all that I did right I learned from Frank. What I did wrong was because I wasn't a better student.

An experience he and I shared away from the court happened in 1970 in Charleston, South Carolina. We had worked the Baylor versus Ole Miss game that ended late, and we were both hungry. At about 2:00 a.m., we found a 24-hour "greasy spoon" and went in. I ordered a burger, and Frank ordered a club sandwich.

The place was not that busy. Some 45 minutes later, we still had not been served. From the kitchen came a rather large fellow wearing an apron and one of those white hats with our order in his hand.

He asked which one of us had ordered the club sandwich. I'm not so sure either one of us wanted to answer, but Frank slowly raised his hand.

"What's a club sandwich?" the cook asked. Frank explained, and a short time later, we got our food.

As the years went by, our friendship grew stronger.

We talked often over the phone after he retired from broadcasting in 1995. When we said good-bye, he never failed to tell me he loved me, and I responded in kind.

Every young up-and-coming broadcaster should be fortunate enough to have a Frank Fallon as a mentor.

As you look down from heaven, Frank, thank you.

## Dave Elmendorf and Al Pulliam

When you broadcast any sport, whether that's football, basketball, or baseball, you need a knowledgeable partner. I've been fortunate to work with two such people in my career at Texas A&M: Dave Elmendorf in football and Al Pulliam in basketball.

Both played for Texas A&M. Dave was a football and baseball player and academic All-American. When he finished at Texas A&M, he was drafted by the Los Angeles Rams and the New York Yankees.

Al had the opportunity to play for the legendary Shelby Metcalf and then to serve as an academic advisor in athletics. He then joined the Texas A&M Foundation and still works in corporate and foundation relations. Al wasn't just a smart, reliable broadcast partner; he also was a trusted adviser to young athletes. Student athletes would seek him out, and parents and relatives with young men seeking guidance about their futures would ask for his insight. He loves the game of basketball, and he is passionate about young men making good choices and growing into responsible adults.

I always had confidence that both Dave and Al would say the right thing. They just tell you what happened, support the coaches, and never criticize a player.

One more note on Dave Elmendorf: In December 2017, the Touchdown Club of Houston honored me with the Ron Stone Media Achievement Award. I was asked to select someone to introduce me, and I chose Dave.

He went way, way above and beyond. He knew that my broadcast hero was Vin Scully, the man I believe to be the greatest announcer to ever speak into a microphone. Scully also happened to have been the voice of the Dodgers for 67 years before retiring in 2016.

Dave contacted the Los Angeles Dodgers, told them about the award, and asked if they could get Vin Scully to record a congratulations message. And they did!

The Dodgers sent a 59-second video for the dinner that night. Vin Scully sent his congratulations, saluted my retirement, and wished me well in my continued work with Aggie baseball. After the event, our granddaughter, Gianna, walked up to me and said, "Poppy, Vin Scully knows your name!"

Dave, as I told you that night, what you did blew me away!

## Wally Groff

I had the honor of working with Wally Groff when he was CFO and athletics director.

Wally had numerous strengths, which allowed him to excel in both roles at Texas A&M, but the two strengths I recognized more than any other were his love for Texas A&M and his loyalty to those who worked in the athletic department.

Wally had an open-door policy, and he would make time for anyone in the department to discuss whatever was on their mind.

There was a time when staff who had 10 plus years of service were presented with a "Letterman's Ring." I will never forget the staff meeting when Wally presented me with mine. There was some disagreement within the department about staff members being awarded a ring, but earning that ring meant a lot to me.

When I retire totally from Texas A&M, I will have seen more sporting events than anyone in the history of the university. Leanne and I have also been blessed to give back to the 12th Man Foundation. I know earning a Letterman's Ring was special to other staff, too. I hope that Wally didn't get criticized for something that meant a lot to a lot of folks.

I got a call one day, and when the man gave his class year, I figured him to be at least 85 years old. He wanted the television schedule for the upcoming season. When I told him it would be at least 30 days before it was released, he blew up. He started cussing and telling me I wasn't doing my job, or I would force the powers-to-be to release it right then.

I started laughing, and he asked what I was laughing about. I said his cussing reminded me of my grandad Charlie and brought back some good memories.

He asked, "I'm not making you mad, am I?" He said he wanted to make someone mad, so I gave him Wally's number. I told him that if he called that number and talked to that person like he did to me, he'd make that person mad.

I waited about 30 minutes and then walked down to Wally's office. I asked if an older gentleman call him about the television schedule, and he said yes.

"Did he cuss at you?" Wally said yes.

"Did you get back in his face?" Again, Wally said yes.

"Good, you made his day!"

## John David Crow

During my time at A&M, I had the honor of traveling with the late John David Crow, Texas A&M's former athletics director.

More often than not, someone would come up and ask John David how tough it was at Junction (Bear Bryant's brutal summer training camp in 1954.). He would always reply that he didn't go to Junction because he was an incoming freshman. But they wouldn't believe John David! They would say that he did go but just didn't want to talk about it.

After a few of these encounters, we were at Aggie Park in San Antonio when a gentleman walked up and asked how tough the workouts were at Junction. John David said they were tough, which seemed to make the man happy, and he walked away. John David looked at me and said he was tired of arguing with them!

The other comment John David would get was from fans saying they would like to see an Aggie team from John David's playing days play one of current Aggie squads.

John David would look at the fan and say he thought that would be interesting. When the fan was out of earshot, he would look at me and say that one of the current teams would kill any of his teams from the 1950s.

## John Kimbrough

I never met Mr. Kimbrough but wish I had. I did get to talk to him, though, and because of his legacy, I wanted to include this story. I also think this episode showed a side of John David Crow others might not have seen.

Texas A&M celebrated 100 years of Aggie football in 1994. I was assigned to get the autograph of every Aggie consensus All-American for a commemorative football.

For the players who had passed, I searched out living relatives. One found a check that the player had signed. Another found the Texas A&M scholarship paperwork the athlete had signed to confirm his intent to play football for the Aggies.

Getting the autographs of the living All-Americans was easy and just took one phone call. One of those phone calls was to the great John Kimbrough, who was living in Haskell at the time. Kimbrough, an outstanding running back on the Aggies' 1939 national championship team, was known as the "Haskell Hurricane." In 1940, he finished second to Tom Harmon in Heisman Trophy balloting.

Originally, he had planned to attend Tulane University in New Orleans. It seems Tulane had promised Kimbrough's brother a job on campus but rescinded the offer after they arrived. Since school had not started, Kimbrough called Homer Norton, then the head football coach at Texas A&M. Kimbrough's brother was given a job in the dining hall on the A&M campus and "Jarrin'" John transferred to play for the Aggies. The rest is history.

I explained what I was doing, and he said he would be glad to send his autograph. As I was about to hang up, I said, "I guess you get back to College Station a lot." He said he had never been back because they had fired his coach. I asked, "Homer Norton?" He said yes. I mentioned that

*Texas A&M head baseball coach Mark Johnson standing at home plate going over the ground rules. This was prior to our first game in 1999 against Florida State. The Seminoles' head coach is there with Coach Johnson and the umpires: home plate Randy Bruns, first base Rich Fetchiet, second base Tim Norman, and third base Bill Davis.* (Photo Courtesy of Glen Johnson)

*Little Broadcaster Ashton Brown was under a year old at the time. That headset was almost bigger than he was.*

*Friday, November 26, 1999—Thanksgiving weekend. Texas A&M and Texas at Kyle Field. Aggies win, 20–16. The toughest, most emotional game I ever called as a broadcaster.*

*There was never a time that I didn't get chills when the Fightin' Texas Aggie Band marched out onto Kyle Field.* (Photo Courtesy of Glen Johnson)

Joseph Jones grew up in Normangee, a small Texas town near Bryan-College Station. He played basketball for the Aggies from 2005 to 2008. During that time, the Aggies traveled to New York to play at Madison Square Garden. I was walking with Joseph near our hotel and asked him what he thought about New York City. His reply: "This isn't Normangee."

Former Aggie head baseball coach Mark Johnson on August 8, 2018. Mark and I share the same birthday. We were celebrating our 73rd in this picture. Mark coached Texas A&M baseball from 1985 to 2005 and coached at Sam Houston State from 2007 to 2011. He won 1,042 total games as a collegiate head coach.

*Looking over my shoulder from the broadcast booth in Kyle Field. No matter what the score of the game, it's always an impressive view.*

*This is Andrew Monaco, who was named the new Aggie football and basketball play-by-play announcer in June 2018. Andrew and I met to exchange ideas on broadcasting in August shortly after my 73rd birthday. Andrew has a great personality, and I have no doubt he will do a great job and that Aggie fans will welcome him!*

*Chuck Glenewinkel is a former Texas A&M sports information director. Chuck worked with me to broadcast the Aggie baseball team. At this writing, Chuck works for the College Station Independent School District as the public information director. I've seen Chuck become a husband (to his wife, Lacy) and the father of two sons (Eric and Charlie). A professional in all that he does, Chuck and I shared something that I believe to be a gift from God: a wonderful sense of humor.*

*A typical spotter board, used during the broadcast to quickly associate player statistics by number and position. I constantly tinkered with the layout and design, trying to find the right "fit."*

*From left to right: Brad Marquardt, Alan Cannon associate athletics director media relations and Hall of Fame member; Jackie Thornton, senior office associate; Douglas Walker, senior associate athletics director for external affairs; and me.*

*Texas A&M head baseball coach Rob Childress. Rob took over the program in 2006, which was the only year the team did not go to the NCAAs. As of the completion of the 2018 season, the Aggies had played in 12 consecutive NCAA post-season tournaments, which is a school record. You can also add in the 2011 and 2017 CWS.*

*This photo was taken after the Fall Dinner of the Federation of Texas A&M Mothers' Clubs, held on August 24, 2018, at the Clayton Williams Alumni Center. These ladies were part of the leadership team for the Coppell Aggie Moms' Club. They exemplify the passionate commitment of any and every Aggie mom I met during my tenure at Texas A&M. Left to right: Kris Keever*

*Smith '87, Lisa Armstrong, Dolores Kelly '85, me, Tamra Walker '89, and Sheila Bedichek.*

I am indebted to Linda Hill for the honor she presented to me in April 2003. Linda was the president of the Texas A&M Mothers' Club from 2003 to 2004, and she dedicated the club's yearbook to me. This is a signature honor, and the presentation included a Benjamin Knox print. This was the first real honor I received from an organization associated with Texas A&M. Aggie moms will forever hold a special place in my heart. Left to right: Linda Hill, me, and Benjamin Knox.

Left to right: Byran Farris, me, and Mike Lednicky. Byran and Mike worked as my spotters for several seasons.

The National Football Foundation presented me with the Chris Schenkel Award prior to the Texas A&M–LSU football game on November 24, 2018. This is the description from the NFF website: "Each year, the National Football Foundation and College Hall of Fame presents an award to a sports broadcaster who has had a long and distinguished career broadcasting college football. The award seeks to recognize broadcasters with direct ties to college and universities rather than strictly national broadcasters." Mr. Ron Dilatush of the NFF was on hand to present the award in a pregame ceremony. Leanne and I went to New York on December 4, 2018, for the official awards banquet. This was truly a special moment in my career.

*The plaque I am holding was presented the first time in pregame before the Texas A&M–LSU football game in November 2018. The official presentation was made in New York City on December 4, 2018, at the Hilton Midtown. There were 1,600 in attendance, and the event for all who were recognized was very special. All photos from this event were provided by the National Football Foundation.*

*These three men came to New York to be present when I was given the Chris Schenkel Award. Left to right: Brad Marquardt, Dave Elmendorf, me, and Alan Cannon. I want to thank Brad for nominating me for the award. All photos from this event were provided by the National Football Foundation.*

*National Football Foundation Awards ceremony, December 2018. I had the pleasure of sitting with the athletic directors from Yale, Tom Beckett (left; 1994–2018) and Harvard AD Bob Scalise (middle; 2001–present). All photos from this event were provided by the National Football Foundation.*

*Making the trip to New York was made even more special because my wife and best friend Leanne was invited to attend. All photos from this event were provided by the National Football Foundation.*

*Representing all the Aggie fans in New York was Terry Klein, a longtime A&M donor and good friend for many years. All photos from this event were provided by the National Football Foundation.*

*Our granddaughter Gianna in December of 2017 when the Houston Touchdown Club presented me with the Ron Stone Media Achievement Award*

*Leanne and I in New York for the presentation of the Chris Schenkel award by the National Football Foundation in December of 2018.*

all those responsible were no longer at Texas A&M, but Kimbrough was still angry about Norton's firing.

I explained that I hated to hear that because there were a lot of people, including me, who would love to meet him.

The conversation really bothered me, so about an hour later I walked down to John David Crow's office (our AD at the time) and told him the story. Crow called Kimbrough and then drove to Haskell and talked him into coming back.

Kimbrough did start coming back to Aggieland, but unfortunately for me, I never got to meet him.

## Dave Hrechkosy (A Wreck' a See)

His is not a name a lot of Aggie fans will recognize, but for those of us who got to know him, Dave Hrechkosy was special.

Dave was Texas A&M athletics' concessions director and was outstanding in his duties. He would stop by my office, and we would have long conversations that led to a close friendship.

We discovered early on that we differed politically, so we just never discussed politics. Everyone who knew him would agree that it was easy to be Dave's friend.

Dave, a Canadian, played professional hockey for 11 years. Once he gave me one of his hockey cards that he had autographed and framed. Richard Croome, sportswriter for the *Bryan–College Station Eagle*, also had a close friendship with Dave. When we lost Dave, I gave that framed card to Rich.

Dave was still in charge of concessions when Texas A&M renovated Olsen Field into Blue Bell Park. He called me over one day to show me a sign above one of the concession stands. If you have ever listened to me when the Aggie's hit a home run, I call it a "Big Fly," which is what a lot of baseball scouts call it. There, above the stand, was the name "Big Fly Grill."

We lost Dave Hrechkosy to brain cancer in 2012. He may be gone, but he is not forgotten.

One summer, Leanne and were in San Dimas, California, on vacation. We had taken our dog, Chloe, to a dog park, and I struck up a conversation with a fellow who also was there with his dog.

I asked where he was from, and he said originally Niagara Falls but later Salt Lake City. His father had been a lifelong employee at Coca Cola. Texas A&M had hired Dave from Coca Cola in Salt Lake City. I asked him if he knew Dave Hrechkosy. He responded, "The Wrecker?" That was Dave's nickname when he played hockey. It turns out Dave was his dad's best friend.

I still think of Dave Hrechkosy often and the conversations we shared in my office at Kyle Field.

## Lyle Lovett

Lyle is a Texas A&M former student, and long before I interviewed him, I had almost everything he ever recorded on my iPod. He was on campus to headline a fundraising concert and was performing the next evening at Rudder Auditorium.

I would be hard-pressed to name anyone else who could match this man's humility. I was a fan and excited about just the two of us sharing a microphone and talking for 15 minutes.

He shared his love for Texas A&M, his career, and his music. One of the questions I asked was if he would ever consider coming back to Aggieland and teaching a music class of some kind.

His response was, "Oh, I couldn't do that. I'm still learning myself." Lyle Lovett's interview is one of the few during my career that I have saved.

## Dolly Parton

My interview with Dolly Parton took place when I worked for a radio/television station in Waco. On the way to work that morning, I had stopped by a music store to drop off my guitar to have it restrung and tuned. I picked it up right after lunch, and because it was summer, and I took it into the station instead of leaving it in the car.

When I walked into the lobby, there sat Dolly Parton. She was there to record an interview for the local evening news. When she saw the guitar, she asked if she could use it during the interview. Of course I said yes, and then I asked if she would do an interview with me for the morning news show on the radio.

She was a delightful person, just like you see on television . . . friendly, outgoing, and very down to earth. Looking back, I wish I had asked her to autograph the guitar.

## Pee Wee Reese

Earlier in this book, I talked about my love for the Brooklyn then the Los Angeles Dodgers baseball team. In 1977 and 1978, I was privileged to broadcast games at the College World Series (CWS) in Omaha, Nebraska. One of the events that took place during the CWS was the Fellowship of Christian Athletes Breakfast.

In 1978, former Dodgers shortstop Pee Wee Reese was the featured speaker, and I was there.

When the breakfast ended, Pee Wee agreed to sign autographs. I was in line, and every time someone moved in behind me, I would step out and move to the back of the line until finally, I was the only one left.

I told him how in 1955 at the age of 10, I became a Brooklyn Dodgers fan. That was the only year Brooklyn won a World Series, so I picked a good year! He asked me what I did, and I told him I was a broadcaster. He asked what I was going to do next. I said go back to the room and back to bed.

Then he asked, "Would I like to go to the restaurant and drink some coffee?"

What do you think I said?

For well over an hour, we talked about the Dodgers in Brooklyn and Los Angeles, his broadcast career with Dizzy Dean, and his time as a coach with the Dodgers.

I asked him about the game of baseball when he first started playing and when he finally hung it up as a coach. He said that in his playing days, when the game ended, especially on the road, the players would stay in the locker room and review the game, both the good and the bad parts.

When he hung it up as a coach, he said those players would dress and leave the locker room as quickly as possible. When he played, they had an expression, "First out of the clubhouse, first out of the league."

When I speak to groups of businessmen and salesmen, I use that story. You need to be a student of what you do whether in business, sports, or school.

## Rachel Robinson

In 1999, Leanne and I were invited to New York City for Dave Elmendorf's induction into the National Football Foundation Hall of Fame. While there, I looked for some Brooklyn Dodgers memorabilia and found a 1956 World Series ticket. It was the last World Series the Brooklyn Dodgers played in and the last year that Jackie Robinson played for the Dodgers. He was traded to the Giants at the end of that season but refused the trade and retired.

I bought the ticket, tucked it in my pocket, and kept with me when I went to the banquet. I was among a group from Texas A&M who attended to see Dave be inducted and remember how happy I was for him to receive the honor.

As I was looking at everyone sitting on the stage, I saw former Baylor coach and friend Grant Teaff. There was a lady sitting beside Grant, and at first, I didn't recognize her. The program said she was Rachel Robinson, the widow of my favorite Dodger, Jackie Robinson.

When the event ended, I made my way to the stage and got Grant's attention. He came down, and I explained about the ticket and asked if he would ask Mrs. Robinson to sign it.

He went back, handed her the ticket, and pointed to me. Rachel Robinson walked over and sat down on the edge of the stage and spent at least 20 minutes talking to me about Jackie and life in general. I may have been 54 years old when the event started, but when she started walking to the edge of the stage, I felt like a 10-year-old kid again. It was such a thrill to meet the woman behind the courageous man who did so much for the game of baseball and America.

I still have that ticket, and it is in a very safe place.

## Dick Maegle (Mā' gul)

Dick Maegle was a college All-American football player at Rice University in the 1950s who went on to have a successful professional career. An interesting fact about Dick is that he started college when he was 16 years old.

He was All-SWC and an All-American in 1954 and the 10th overall pick in the 1955 NFL draft. He played for the San Francisco 49ers from 1955 to 1960, the Pittsburgh Steelers in 1960, and the Dallas Cowboys in 1961. Dick also played in the Pro Bowl in 1955.

I worked with Dick Maegle on selected football broadcasts for the SWC Radio Network in the early '80s.

Dick was involved in one of the most bizarre college football plays in history. It happened at the 1954 Cotton Bowl when Rice played Alabama. With Rice leading 7–6, Maegle broke through on a sweep from Rice's 5-yard line and was running down the sideline in front of Alabama's bench on his way to a touchdown. Alabama's Tommy Lewis, without putting on his helmet, jumped off the bench and tackled Maegle. Seeing what happened, Referee Cliff Shaw awarded a 95-yard touchdown on the play, and Rice went on to win the game, 28–6. Dick finished with 265 rushing yards, a Cotton Bowl record until 2008.

At dinner one night, I asked him what went through his head on that play.

"I was running down the sideline in front of the Alabama bench, looked back over my left shoulder at the open field, and no one was there," Maegle said. "Then, looking back at the end zone, the next thing I knew, someone hit me from behind. I went down and thought, 'That has to be the fastest man in the world.'"

Years later, at a Cotton Bowl luncheon in Dallas, I sat down at an open table next to a fellow and introduced myself. It was Tommy Lewis, the Alabama player who had tackled Dick in 1954.

I couldn't keep from smiling when he said, "Yes, I'm that Tommy Lewis." I explained my relationship with Dick Maegle. I feel honored to have met both men involved in that famous play.

## Bobby and Woody

Two coach interviews that stand out for me were done with Woody Hayes and Bobby Knight.

The first was with Coach Hayes in Columbus, Ohio, sometime in the 1970s. Then the SWC owned the rights for radio and assigned broadcasters to work the various games each Saturday. I had been assigned the SMU–Ohio State game, and we were doing pregame interviews with opposing coaches at the time, so I scheduled an interview with Hayes at the end of the Buckeyes' walkthrough on Friday afternoon.

Keep in mind that Coach Hayes was known for his temper. I remembered the 1971 Michigan game, when he grabbed the down box from a member of the chain gang and threw it onto the edge of the field. Most folks remember the 1978 Gator Bowl game against Clemson, when a livid Hayes threw a punch at the Tigers' Charlie Bauman on the sideline after Bauman intercepted a pass late in the game.

I was in my late 20s and was not looking forward to the interview. After practice ended, I walked over and introduced myself. He said, "You have two minutes."

Was I nervous? Yes! How nervous? My hand was shaking so badly that he grabbed my hand with the microphone in it and held it the entire interview. When the interview was over, I said thank you and walked away without comment. I know my voice cracked a couple of times.

I don't remember the exact circumstances of the Bobby Knight interview except that I was the A&M broadcaster, and Coach Metcalf and the Aggies had ended up at an event with Knight's Indiana Hoosiers. Metcalf and Knight had a common interest that went past basketball: a love of fishing.

I needed a pregame interview with Knight. Shelby asked him for me, and he said yes. We talked for at least six minutes. It couldn't have gone any better. Every question drew a well thought out response. When it ended, he said thank you, shook my hand, and walked away.

The recorder was on the floor between my feet. I bent down to hit the stop button, only to find I never started it. I was not about to yell across the floor and say, "Coach, can you come back and let's do it for real?"

## Corporal Matthew Bradford, USMC (Retired)

In 2013, the University of Kentucky made their first trip to College Station to play the Aggies at Reed Arena. The Aggies lost in overtime, 72–68.

This game was special to me because I met Matt Bradford.

Before the game started, I was asked if I had a radio for a Kentucky fan who was at the game that day. I did not have a radio but instead invited him to sit between Al and me during the game. He accepted, and as the game moved along, I visited with Matt during the time-outs.

Matt was married, and he and his wife had a child. Matt was a marine and grew up going to Kentucky games with his grandfather. He told me that it had always been his dream to do the play-by-play for Wildcat basketball.

When the game ended, Matt presented me with a coin that included the Marine Corps logo. We made plans for Matt to join us the next season when Texas A&M played Kentucky at Rupp Arena.

In 2007, while deployed in Iraq, Matt stepped on a roadside bomb. The resulting injuries cost him his eyesight, both legs at the knees, and use of an arm.

He has been quoted saying, "Just because I'm blind doesn't mean I don't have vision. I believe God kept me alive for a reason, and that's to tell my story."

When the Aggies visited Lexington in 2014, coach Billy Kennedy invited Matt and his wife to join the team for the team dinner the night before the game.

Knowing his love for Kentucky basketball, I asked Matt to join us on the broadcast Saturday night. We did a scouting report on each team, and Matt gave the report on Kentucky.

When it came time, Matt delivered a poised, in-depth look at the Wildcats. I threw him a curveball and asked a follow-up question, and he handled it like a broadcast veteran.

Matt later appeared on a radio show in Lexington to talk about the Wildcats and the upcoming games on their schedule. Matt Bradford is the reason I finish each broadcast with "God bless our wounded warriors, pray for our wounded warriors."

If you go to the internet and Google Corporal Matthew Bradford, you will find that he graduated from the University of Kentucky in May 2017, has traveled across the country as a motivational speaker, participates in half marathons, has gone skydiving, shared the stage with country singer

Toby Keith, and was a guest of President Trump's at the January 2018 State of the Union address.

Matt, thank you to you and all your fellow soldiers, men and women, for your service.

## Dr. Ed Richards

One of my dearest friends is Dr. Ed Richards. Ed and his wife, Susan, are both A&M former students.

Ed and I first met on a basketball trip to Lincoln, Nebraska.

Ed and I found that we both felt strongly about our walk with Christ. He has a unique perspective on life due to his work as an oncologist—a cancer doctor.

Normally on these plane trips for basketball, I sat with Al Pulliam, our color analyst. On this trip, Al hadn't boarded the plane yet, and a group of Aggie donors who had been invited were making their way down the aisle.

Ed was with this group. He passed by and stopped at the row behind me and then leaned over and asked if the empty window seat next to me was taken. I said yes and that my buddy Al would be sitting there. Ed then took the seat in front of me.

Al entered the plane, and when he got to me, I started to get up so he could get in. He explained that one of the players wanted to visit with him, and he was going to sit with him on the way up to Lincoln.

Hearing that, Ed stood up and asked if he could take that seat, and I said sure. I figured that he wanted to talk Aggie sports, but that wasn't the case.

When he had passed by the first time, Ed had noticed the book in my lap: *Prayer*, by Philip Yancy. He wanted to talk about that book and other aspects of my faith as well as his own.

We spent the flight up, dinner that night, breakfast the next morning, and the flight back discussing Christ, our families, friends, and how God was working in our lives. I also explained the reason for the Philip Yancey book. I was looking for answers on how to pray and what to pray. The Yancey book helped in that search.

There was one more thing that I shared on the trip that I would like to share in this book. I had been to a dentist office and picked up a *National Geographic* to read while I was waiting.

In that issue was a story on World War II and some letters that were shared between husbands and wives separated by the war. In one letter, a husband explained to his wife how she should pray: "Ask God to give you what you want. Help him to justify your wants by the way you live and then, having given him your prayer, have faith and courage to rely on his power to do the thing that is right in his eyes." As I recall, Ed had emailed that quote to his wife and three daughters.

Ed and I still talk but rarely about sports. Our faith and how God is working in our lives is the center of our conversations. On his visits to College Station, we try to work in a breakfast or lunch and more times of sharing.

One of our more meaningful times together was in New York City for a basketball game at Madison Square Garden. However, it was not the games but the mass we attended at Saint Patrick's Cathedral.

He shared an outlook that every fan should adopt: "Let the coaches coach, let the players play, let the administrators be administrators, let the broadcasters be broadcasters, and let the fans be fans."

Just enjoy the game and support your team. When the game is over, it's over. We should all move on to what is next in our lives.

When you listen to the radio broadcast of Aggie baseball, you will hear me say, "Coming to you from the Richards Family Home Radio Booth." This recognizes Ed and his family for their gift for the renovation of Olsen Field into Blue Bell Park.

If you ever meet Ed Richards, ask him about the time he worked in the radio booth with a very complicated stat page at the Cotton Bowl.

## 2017 South Carolina Game: Aggie Moms

When I first sat down to write the memory moment for this week's game, I was going to talk about overtime games during my career, but then something happened: I became an honorary Aggie Mom!

During my 32 years with Texas A&M, I was often asked to speak at different events. One that I always enjoyed was speaking to the Aggie Moms across the state.

These ladies give back unselfishly to the university in raising money for scholarships. Many join when their student starts at Texas A&M. Some join after that student has graduated. Whenever these mothers join, they get busy raising funds to help students.

One of their many activities, and one of the most fun to attend, is the Aggie Mom's Boutique on Family Weekend. During finals, they pass out goodie bags to students in the Memorial Student Center.

For two years in a row, I emceed a Houston-area Aggie Moms gathering, helping with what they called a crazy auction. To this day, I have no idea how it worked, but I know it raised a lot of money, and we had a blast.

In 2003, Linda Hill was the president of the Federation of Aggie Mothers' Clubs, and she presented me with a special honor, their yearbook dedication.

In August 2017, I was invited to a meeting of the Brazos County Aggie Moms by their president, Cindy DeWitt. Something happened that I will remember for the rest of my life. I became the first male to be designated an Honorary Aggie Mom for Brazos County. Thank you, Cindy, board members, and members of the Brazos County Aggie Moms.

The Federation of Texas A&M University Mothers' Clubs, 6,000 strong in more than 100 clubs have one common goal: to band together to do whatever is necessary to benefit the students at Texas A&M University. Aggie Moms are truly a special group of women.

Thank you to all the Aggie Moms across the nation.

# 9

# Places

Most of these events are associated with a game or event, but not all. Still, they all took place in a stadium or arena or field, so we decided to categorize these stories by their location, hence the title of this chapter, "Places." Might as well get my most infamous moment as a broadcaster out of the way first, so here it is.

## Reunion Arena

### March 12, 1993

### Houston 84–Texas A&M 68

The rule for fan behavior is addressed in the rule book covering college basketball. The rule states that "a fan may be removed from the stands if said fan is interfering with the play of game."

The 1993 SWC basketball season brought about the worst officiating perhaps ever for the league. Evidence of that came at the end of that season, when the director of officiating was removed along with several officials.

It was rare for the media to comment or write about basketball officials. However, leading into the 1993 SWC tournament, the *Houston Post* (no longer printed) did an article on basketball officiating in the SWC. It was rather critical, citing some coaches' negative opinions and even calling out certain officials by name for poor performance.

So there was a cloud hanging over the tournament. The Aggies played the Houston Cougars in a first-round game, and by halftime, the calls averaged about 2 to 1 against the Aggies in a game where their opponent played a physical style of basketball.

There is a protocol for officials during a time-out. With a three-man crew, attention should be given to the two benches and the scorer's table. The officials standing at each end of the floor were to watch the team bench while the official at the midcourt line watched the scorer's table.

At some point in the second half, a time-out was called on the floor. I was working the game with our sports information director Colin Killian, and we had gone to a commercial break.

The official at the end of the floor where we were broadcasting from had placed himself directly in front of me at the free-throw line instead of being turned toward the team. Unlike most games that season, we were not situated courtside but were back on the second row of broadcast tables.

At first, I couldn't tell if the official was looking at me or if he had one of those blank stares that we all have from time to time. I looked at the other sideline where Houston coach Pat Foster was talking to his team.

When I glanced back, the official was in the same spot, and it became apparent that he was looking at me. I had a soft drink in my left hand and lifted it to give him a toast and with my right hand gestured to him with a quick choke sign to my throat. That took about five seconds.

The official turned and went to the baseline and returned with a security guard to our sideline and started yelling at me that I was gone. I told Colin he would have to take it the rest of the way.

We were still in a time-out, and Houston had a big lead over Texas A&M. When I got up to leave, it seemed like almost all the media on press row followed me off the floor.

I immediately asked to see our athletics director John David Crow. With the security guard at my side, John David and I moved away from the media, and I explained what happened. I will always be grateful that he stood by me in that circumstance. John David told me to go with the security guard, and he would handle the press.

The guard took me out of the arena. As we approached the door, I stopped and asked to talk to a conference official. I explained that when the game ended, I had the right to go back down and do our postgame show. I could tell the official wanted no part of what was going on. He went across from where the three of us were standing and radioed back down to the floor. When he returned, he said I was to be locked in a room adjacent to the floor, and when the game ended, I could return to the floor to finish the broadcast.

When we got back down to the floor level, the room where I was to be held was in front of the tunnel leading back to the court. Coming out of that tunnel was Tom Penders, the Texas Longhorn head coach. He walked up, gave me a big hug, and whispered, "You are my new hero."

The ejection was the main story from the SWC tournament on Sports Center for the rest of the night. Colin and I were joined by friends for dinner. The waiter taking our order looked at me and then at the television nearby and said, "You're the guy that got kicked out of the game."

Later, the comic strip "Tank McNamara" would do a week on what had happened that day at the game. The fellow who did the strip sent me the artwork in a nice frame with the inscription "To Dave South, an Inspiration" written across the top.

There is a desk calendar that comes out each year called "The Sports Hall of Shame," and every so often someone will send me the page on my ejection.

Fast forward to the Big 12 Basketball tournament one year when it was played at American Airlines Arena in Dallas.

After the A&M game, I was standing by our locker room waiting for the coach so I could follow him to the postgame press conference room.

I was leaning against the wall near a security guard. We started talking, and he asked who I was with, and I said Texas A&M. He began to tell me about a time when the A&M radio broadcaster had been ejected from a game at Reunion Arena.

I said, "Really? Tell me about it."

He went through the story as he remembered it. When he finished, I told him that's not what happened. He said, "I guess it is; I was the security guard that took him off the court," to which I replied, "Well, I'm the announcer you took off the court."

He started laughing and asked me to tell him exactly what happened. When I finished, he asked me to stay right there and walked away. When he returned, he had another security guard with him and asked if he could get his picture with me.

One final note on this story: At the 2016 NCAA Basketball Tournament in Oklahoma City, Texas A&M beat the University of Wisconsin–Green Bay, 92–65, in the first round. Green Bay's announcer, Matt Menzl, had been temporarily ejected from his team's conference tournament only to be allowed to return a short time later to finish the game.

Matt and I talked and laughed about the shared experience. Then he asked me when the buzz would die down and people would stop talking about it.

I said, "Never."

## Billy Pickard and the Yellow Spot

You couldn't work around Kyle Field and not know Billy Pickard. Pickard was a former student who worked as a student athletic trainer under Bear Bryant and was later hired to return to Texas A&M by Gene Stallings.

He would later become an associate athletic director in charge of facilities. Absolutely nothing at Kyle Field went unchecked by Pickard. Before the start of every football season, he would flush every commode and urinal in the stadium and check all the bleacher bench seats to make sure they were securely bolted in place.

Pickard and I played many rounds of golf together. At Kyle Field, if you got on his bad side, he would let you have it like a Marine Corps drill sergeant. On the golf course, if he hit a bad shot, his only comment would be "I'm glad I don't know any bad words." Believe me, he knew a lot of bad words, but not while playing golf.

One summer during the mid-1990s, Andy Richardson (currently assistant athletic director for 12th Man Productions) and his staff came up with an idea for a commercial called "Dog Days of Summer" to promote the upcoming football season.

The spot featured Reveille, the Aggie mascot, and four of her "friends" running onto Kyle Field with the caption "Aggie football is coming."

On the day of the shoot, I arrived early with our Australian Shepard Katie. We walked around outside the stadium so she could take care of her business before going inside.

Once on the field, I took her off her leash and let her run around. Then it happened: she relieved herself on the sideline at about the 50-yard line. My cell phone rang. It was Pickard.

"Whose #$%@#&* dog is that?" he asked.

I replied that it was mine.

"You know your #$%@#&* dog just peed on the field?"

I apologized, saying I didn't think that would happen, since she had also done her business before we entered the stadium.

"Well, get her off the field right now!" he suggested with vigor.

Reveille and the other dogs had not arrived yet, so I explained what we were doing. There were more choice words and a comment about what he would do to the next dog that did anything to the grass.

I never knew where he was calling from, nor did he come out to the shoot. Much to my relief, we finished without any more phone calls.

Fast forward to the hours before the first football game of the season. I was in the radio booth getting ready for the broadcast when my phone rang. It was Pickard. I answered, he asked if I was in the press box, and I said yes.

"Look down on the field. Can you see me?" Pickard was standing on the sideline at about the 50-yard line.

He told me to look down by his right foot.

Pickard asked, "Can you see the yellow spot?"

I could.

"That's where your damn dog peed on the field."

The spot was about where Coach Slocum would stand for every home game. So when I looked at R. C., my eyes would drop to that yellow spot.

Pickard called me before every home game that year. I would look down and see him, answer the phone, and say, "I see it!"

His response was always the same: "Thank you, sir."

When I visited Pickard in his office, he would always say the same thing as I got up to leave: "Come back when you can't stay so long!"

We lost Billy on March 9, 2015. I wish he could have stayed longer.

## Cain Dining Hall and Beanie Wienies

Here is another Billy Pickard story, this time involving Cain Dining Hall.

At one time, Billy helped with campus visits during football recruiting. One of his responsibilities was working with the staff at Cain Dining Hall on the meal.

During a surprise visit with a highly regarded recruit, Billy got an unexpected call asking for lunch at noon with steak, baked potatoes, salad, veggies, and a good dessert. He rushed over to Cain Hall only to learn that there were no steaks and not enough time to go buy everything requested for the meal. Billy asked what was on the menu for that day and almost fainted when he was told it was beanie wienies.

At noon, in walked three or four coaches, the recruit, his dad, and his high school coach. Billy tried not to make eye contact with the coach, and when he did, all he got was an icy stare.

When the recruit left, Billy tried to explain what had happened, but all the coach said was that Pickard had likely cost Texas A&M that player. If you knew Billy, you knew that he was sick about this for weeks.

Lo and behold, on signing day, the recruit signed with Texas A&M. When the freshmen reported in August, Billy saw the young man in the locker room. He explained how the young man had almost cost him his job, and then Pickard asked why he had signed with the Aggies. The young man said it was because of all the research the Aggies had done on him.

Billy asked, "What research?"

The young man said, "How you guys found out my favorite meal was 'beanie wienies!'"

## Tiger Stadium in Baton Rouge

In 1988, Texas A&M would travel to Baton Rouge to play the LSU Tigers. Like Kyle Field, Tiger Stadium has a good home-field atmosphere.

This game would be played on Saturday, September 3, and LSU would shut out the Aggies, 27–0. This was the season that the network added a pregame feature called "Fan in the Stands."

At Kyle Field, I simply took a long mic cord into the stands in front of the press box and selected two or three fans. The idea was to have each of them to express their feelings about the team and the game.

We revived this feature from time to time through the years and during my last season in 2017.

At Tiger Stadium, I had to take a recorder to the area where the Aggie fans held tickets, across the field from the press box in the southeast corner. I would ask one fan to talk about the game from the week before and the game that day. On this day, I found Jerry Fontenot's father.

Jerry Fontenot was born in Lafayette, Louisiana, so he and his family understood Louisiana culture and their love of Tiger football. Jerry was taken in the third round of the 1989 NFL draft by the Chicago Bears. He would play NFL football from 1989 to 2004 and then coach in the NFL from 2006 to 2015.

We found a good spot away from the traffic flow of the fans coming and going and started taping the interview. As long as someone talks into the microphone, it will not pick up anything else. I asked my first question, and as soon as Mr. Fontenot started to talk, a man walked up behind me with the smell of alcohol on his breath.

He began to tell me with very strong language what the Tigers were going to do the Aggies and what he was going to do to me. Mr. Fontenot did not miss a beat. He just kept talking about the game.

Suddenly, in mid-speech, it sounded like he gagged and went silent.

When we finished the interview, I ask Mr. Fontenot what had happened. He said a Louisiana state trooper came up behind the inebriated LSU fan, grabbed him a choke hold, and dragged him away.

At the end of each game that year, Coach Sherrill and I would do a live postgame radio show over the network. We took calls, and the coach would answer questions about the game.

This meant that the team would go on to the airport, and the coach and I would get a ride with local police or a state trooper.

When we finished, I walked out to a state trooper car, got in the front seat, and told the trooper that Coach Sherrill was on his way.

The trooper asked if I was interviewing an Aggie fan before the game, and I said yes.

He mentioned the LSU fan who was cussing me out and then said, "I was hoping he would hit you."

I said that was a strange thing for a law enforcement officer to say.

"Oh, now don't get me wrong. That guy has been around for a few years and is always drunk," the trooper replied. "If he hits you, I could hit him. I hate that guy!"

## LSU Security Guard

Our radio booth for the Texas A&M–LSU football game in Baton Rouge on September 29, 1990, was just a couple of doors down from the A&M coaches booth in the press box at Tiger Stadium. We had just gone into a commercial break when O'Neill Gilbert, a former nose tackle and then graduate assistant for football under Coach Slocum, came into our booth.

I turned around, and Gilbert said they needed help in the coaches' booth. A man kept opening the door and yelling at the coaches and ridiculing Texas A&M, distracting them so much that they couldn't do their jobs. I suggested to Gilbert that he go get security, and he said, "Mr. South, it is the security guard!"

At the next commercial break, I hurried down to their booth and saw the security guard, who turned out to be a deputy sheriff who was larger than Gilbert. When I walked up to him, I could smell alcohol.

I introduced myself and then threatened to bring LSU officials over to his station, noting that when they smelled the alcohol, he would likely lose his job. After this, he calmed down and left the coaches alone.

The Tigers upset the No. 10 Aggies, 17–8.

## Strange Night in Waco

In January 1992, Tony Barone was in his first year as Texas A&M's basketball coach. The team was in Waco on a Saturday to play Baylor at the Ferrell Center. The Aggies would win only six games that year, and one of those six would be against the Bears.

Before the game ever started, a Texas cold front blew in that led to a very serious, and almost deadly, accident. The wind from the cold front somehow caused a vent in the Ferrell Center to close. This vent allowed carbon monoxide to escape into the air outside.

With the vent closed, the carbon monoxide was forced into the Aggie locker room and the locker room used by the referees. (This problem was quickly corrected after this incident.)

Before the game, I went into the locker room and visited with Coach Barone. When I returned to the floor, I sat down by my friend Bob Ammon, who handled the stats that night. I sat there for a moment and wondered what was wrong with the lighting. They seemed to be coming and going, and I felt light-headed.

Bob asked what was wrong with the Aggies. The team was going through a pregame passing drill, but they couldn't catch or pass the ball. Then players started collapsing.

Someone near the tunnel at the north end yelled that there was a gas leak and everybody needed to exit the arena. Baylor maintenance raised a garage door at the end of the tunnel to allow the wind from the cold front to blow in.

Our trainer, Mike "Radar" Ricke, rushed to our locker room and found that assistant coach Mitch Buonaguro had turned blue and was passed out on the floor. Radar dragged him out of the locker room into the hall and applied mouth to mouth until Buonaguro revived.

Meanwhile, someone from Baylor rushed to the referees' locker room, where two officials were dizzy, and one had passed out. They were taken out into the tunnel, where EMS personnel took over.

One ambulance after another started arriving to transport our team, Buonaguro, and the three referees to local hospitals. Colin Killian, our basketball sports information director, and I were walking toward the garage door when he collapsed and had to be taken to the hospital.

Everyone was spread out over two hospitals. Upon arrival, blood was drawn to determine how much carbon monoxide was in our systems. If the number reading was 17 or more, you were put on pure oxygen until the level dropped below 17.

By 4:00 am, all but four were cleared to leave. The bus arrived back on campus at about 6:00 am. Colin told me that about seven people were taken to Dallas, where they were placed in a hyperbaric chamber. Those from A&M were Colin, player Anthony Ware, Buonaguro, and another assistant coach, John Pigatti. My blood reading registered an 18, so I was given oxygen for about an hour before I was released.

There wasn't much about this in the media, but that was understandable. By the time the storyline of the incident began to take shape, deadlines for newspaper and television had passed. No one from A&M was available to talk on Sunday, so it would be Monday before the full story came to light.

Those in Dallas would return by Tuesday and were cleared to go back to work. The game was played later in February, and the Aggies won it.

Two notes: Some 30 days after the incident, I got a letter from one of the hospitals that treated most of the team. Since I had lived in Waco for a few years, many of the people there knew me, so I was the likely candidate to get the bill.

Inside was an invoice for $125,000 with my name on it. I showed the bill to our CFO Wally Groff, and he advised me to call the president of Baylor. I knew him personally, and he couldn't have been more apologetic. Baylor took care of the bill.

When we played the game in February, several Aggie students came up from campus and wore gas masks from tip-off to final buzzer.

## Savannah, Georgia, and Aggie Marines

In 1996, the A&M basketball went to Savannah, Georgia, to play Georgia Southern. Savannah is a beautiful city. Being the Aggie broadcaster allowed me the opportunity to travel with Aggie teams to some wonderful places, and Savannah is right up there as one of the best.

At the game that night, three families wearing Aggie gear walked into the civic center downtown. When we were on the road, if I saw Aggie fans in the stands, I tried to go and meet them. Turns out the men were Aggies *and* marines stationed at a marine air base nearby.

The team took the floor for pregame warm-up and then left and returned to the locker room. As they got ready to reenter the floor, two fellows wearing Texas Longhorn shirts positioned themselves on either side of the walkway. As the team ran by, they yelled, "Hook 'em horns" until everyone had passed by.

When the game started, these two men sat behind the Aggie bench and started heckling the players and the bench. During time-outs, they moved right behind the bench and yelled. Finally, right before halftime, head coach Tony Barone moved the team onto the floor and away from the bench so he could talk to the players.

At halftime, A&M's sports information director Colin Killian asked officials to remove the two men from behind the bench, and they moved the men up into the stands. They continued their heckling in the second half but could no longer disrupt time-outs.

The Aggies won the game, 67–63. As I packed up my equipment, I saw two of the three Aggie marines hurrying across the floor. I tried to talk to them as they passed by, but they were in a hurry. When they reached their group, they skedaddled out of there.

Once the team and traveling party got on the bus, we drove around the facility on our way back to our hotel. As we approached the other side, we saw an ambulance, police, and flashing lights. One of the Longhorn fans was talking to a police officer; the other one was lying on a stretcher.

Now, I don't know what happened, but I've got an idea.

## Al in Philadelphia

The Aggies had gone to Philadelphia for NCAA postseason basketball in 2009. A&M would play BYU and win 79–66 and then lose to No. 5 Connecticut, 92–66. Mark Turgeon was in his second year as head coach.

The team was staying in a very nice, five-star hotel on the edge of downtown. We could take the train to the arena for the games. The top two or three floors were owned by permanent residents.

This story has nothing to do with the games. It is about my basketball partner Al Pulliam, the color analyst for Aggie basketball. A noise woke him at about 2 a.m. in the morning. He turned on the light in time to see a rat running across the window ledge inside the room.

He got up, got dressed, and went downstairs. At the front desk, he told the clerk on duty that there was a rat in his room.

She asked, "Are you in room 602?" and he said yes.

Then she said, "We've been trying to catch him, but no luck so far."

Pulliam changed rooms.

## Another Strange Night in Waco

There has always been a bit of bad blood between Texas A&M and Baylor. Matters weren't helped by the basketball game in Waco on March 5, 2008.

The Aggies would win the game, 71–57, under then head coach Mark Turgeon.

As the game was winding down with just seconds to play, the Baylor defense had stayed at the far end of the floor with four Aggie players.

Guard Donald Sloan dribbled the ball across the 10-second line and was to let the last few seconds run off. Sloan looked over at my broadcast partner Al Pulliam and me, winked, and then took off to the goal. He threw the ball off the backboard, leaped in the air, grabbed the ball, and slammed it as the buzzer went off, giving us that 71–59 score.

Baylor had given out plastic bottles filled with a soft drink that night as part of a promotion. Bottles started raining down from the stands with some of the caps on the bottles removed. Some came close to press row, but most hit the floor. Turgeon alertly hustled the team off the floor, and the fans ran out of bottles to throw. Then it got interesting.

When broadcasters have their headsets on, they can't hear anything other than their own voices, their producer, and the commercials that are played during time-outs. We had just taken our third commercial break in the postgame when I noticed Baylor coach Scott Drew on a knee holding the PA microphone, leading the arena in prayer.

As I was looking across the floor at Drew, the ESPN broadcast team who sat next to me came back from break and started talking.

There was an older couple sitting right behind us. The wife stood up and started yelling at the ESPN color analyst to be quiet and shoved him in the back.

Still talking and without turning around, he raised his right hand to brush off whoever was pushing him in the back. In doing so, he inadvertently hit the woman on the chin with the back of his hand. She stumbled back but didn't fall. Then the husband got up and started shoving him and telling him he couldn't hit his wife.

We were still in break, so I stood up and asked the husband and wife to sit down. I explained that the ESPN crew was not being rude but that they couldn't hear what was going on because they had on their headsets.

We were just about to go back on the air when ESPN went to break, and the color analyst looked at me and asked who pushed him. I said it had been handled, but then he stood up and at 6'8", looked down at me and asked again. I looked up at him, pointed to the couple, and put my headset back on. To this day I have no idea what happened after that.

By the way, Donald Sloan was still on the team when the Aggies played Baylor the next year. You can imagine the welcome he got that night.

## Mizzou Visiting Baseball Booth

On our first trip to the University of Missouri for a Big 12 baseball series, the visiting radio booth was right above the concession stand. There were quarter-inch spaces in the floorboards. The smoke from the grill would rise and find its way into the booth.

I got on the bus after the first game, and the person sitting beside me asked how many hamburgers I had eaten. My clothes were saturated with the smoke from the patties and the wieners.

## Iowa State Baseball

When we joined the Big 12, we made trips for the first time to several new baseball stadiums.

The Iowa State Cyclones' stadium was the equivalent of a good Texas high school facility, but they played pretty good baseball. But they also had their challenges in fielding their baseball program.

One season, the Aggies played Iowa State in the middle of April at Ames. The Cyclones were playing only their second home series of the year because the other games had been weathered out.

Another time, the Texas Longhorns landed in Des Moines on their way to Ames, and it was snowing. They flew back to Austin.

Fans entered the stadium through a large gate. When it was opened, a sign on the gate said, "Game Today, Free Admission."

One year, with the temperature in the mid-30s, the Oklahoma State broadcaster got permission to pull his car up next to the backstop and did the game from the front seat.

When they finally built the press box, it was half an A-frame with not much room. There was a deck built outside and to the left of home plate. I moved down to the deck, found a folding table, and turned a garbage can upside down for a seat. The weather was good, so I did all three games sitting on the trash can.

I remember standing for the National Anthem and counting the crowd. There were 43 people, including six Aggies.

Our pitching coach then was Jim Lawler. One year, his wife Trish made the trip. When she got back to the hotel, one of their children called and asked her not to talk so loudly because they could hear everything she was saying on the radio!

Iowa State played baseball from 1892 to 2001.

## Dale Mitchell Field in Norman, Oklahoma

Once the mother of a redshirt freshman told me she would do what the other mothers did during the game. I asked what that was. She was going to bring a radio and listen to the broadcast. She wanted to drown out what some people sitting around her were saying about their sons.

You just never know who you are sitting near. I would never want to get crosswise with a mother about her son or daughter.

For example, the Aggies were playing the Oklahoma Sooners in baseball in Norman. Our broadcast booth in the press box was close to the fans, and you could hear everything that was said. A Sooner fan was all over our pitcher, who was having a bad day. This man would not let up, saying one unkind remark after another. That went on for at least three innings.

Suddenly, off to my right came a lady, not walking up an aisle but walking over seats and benches headed for the loudmouth. I recognized her. She was the pitcher's mother. She gave that Sooner fan an earful. He kept moving away from her, but she wouldn't let up. Finally, he just got up and left the stadium.

# The Trains at Baseball Games

If you ever came to an Aggie baseball game, you would see three or more trains pass by on the tracks outside the right field fence.

Currently there is a tall, chain link fence on each side of the tracks to keep people from crossing anywhere along the tracks except at the street crossings at John Kimbrough Boulevard and George Bush Drive.

There was a time when the fence wasn't there. Students would build scaffolding on the side of the tracks near Olsen Field from which to view the games. When safety became an issue, the fence went up, and that vantage point was lost to the ages.

There is a game within the game that fans play when trains pass by going north or south. You can hear the horn as it approaches, but it's not in view of the fans.

When the horn sounds, fans hold up two, three, four, or more fingers, which is their way of telling everyone how many engines they think will pass by.

Almost no one ever picks one because it rarely happens that a train is pulling its load with just one engine. Once a train went by that was just engines, five or six in all.

One night, a big Aggie yell went up when the presidential train for President George H. Bush rolled by. It was easy to spot because it was painted blue and white.

Before the Student Rec Center was built, you could see the train coming from the north as far away as the Albritton Tower intersection, about a quarter mile away.

Many of the train engineers would start sounding out the Aggie War Hymn on the horn.

During one game, you could see the train and hear the Aggie War Hymn being sounded out as everyone was standing for the National Anthem.

As the train neared the stadium, the engineer realized we were honoring the United States. The engine disappeared behind the green monster in center field and then reappeared on the right field side. Standing at attention in the window of the engine was the engineer with his hand on his heart.

There have been a few anxious moments as trains passed by Olsen Field at Blue Bell Park. One evening, someone pulling a trailer was headed east on George Bush. The very end of the trailer was on the edge of the track, and we heard the train hit the trailer. Fortunately, no one was hurt. When the fans heard the loud crash, many rushed to the top of the upper deck to see what had happened. That's the only time I can remember an accident happening during a game.

When the scaffolding was still up, the trains were told to slow down to a snail's pace for fear of someone being hit. One person decided to jump on the train and start waving to the fans in the stadium. The train picked up some speed, and the person couldn't find a spot to jump off.

I was told that they finally got word to the engineer, who stopped in Tomball, where authorities were waiting for the train-hopping student.

There was a loud explosion one night that sounded like multiple shotgun blasts. About half of the cars came uncoupled, and the air hoses pulled apart, causing the gunshot sounds. I found out that night that a train can't stop on a dime. The train engines traveled more than a mile down tracks before stopping. The incident stopped traffic for more than an hour on George Bush Drive, since some of the cars had stopped at the crossover.

One of the funniest sights that I ever saw was a Sunday afternoon game in 2003. There was the sound of the train horn coming from the south. Naturally all the fans started holding up fingers to announce how many engines they thought would pass by.

But instead of a train, Keith Lane and his brother Brent walked by on the tracks with a parade of friends. When I asked Keith about it, he thought there may have been as many as a dozen helping. They had a generator, an air compressor, a train horn, two 16-foot telescoping flag poles, and a tarp strung between the two poles. Keith was in a runoff for yell leader. The tarp sported a sign promoting Keith's election.

That went beyond expectations for creativity—it was as good as it gets for a student election tactic. Now though, the fence and strict laws would prevent that.

By the way, Keith did not win the runoff, but it wasn't for a lack of trying.

Today Keith is married to Katy (class of '02), and they live in College Station with their two children, classes of '30 and '32. If you have seen

Bus 12, you have likely seen the entire Lane family. Keith and his brother Brent built Bus 12, and their father runs it. Bus 12 is in the College Football Hall of Fame, at Aggie home games, and at some road games.

Alan Cannon, our hall-of-fame sports information director, told me this train story that was told to him by former baseball head coach Tom Chandler.

The Aggies were taking batting practice one afternoon, and a train pulling a long string of boxcars passed by. Some of the doors on the boxcars were open.

There was the swing of the bat, and an Aggie hit a bomb. It carried far enough to land in the open door of one of the cars. Coach Chandler said something like, "Men, that will go down as the longest home run in the history of the game."

We were not the only school with trains, but we are the only one I am aware of where fans count engines. Trains also pass by Lindsay Nelson Stadium in Knoxville, Tennessee; Haymarket Park in Lincoln, Nebraska; and Baum Stadium in Fayetteville, Arkansas. The train at Oregon State in Corvallis, Oregon, is unique because it passes through the middle of the campus. You could walk faster than the train could go.

As strange as that may seem, the late Satchel Paige had equally interesting a train story. Paige was playing in a Mexican league game during the off season at a stadium with a gate in the right field corner and a gate in the left field corner. From time to time, the game would stop, and the gates would open so a train could pass from one side to the other.

That certainly gave a new meaning to "warning track."

## G. Rollie White Coliseum

My first office at Texas A&M was in G. Rollie White Coliseum. G. Rollie was the home for men's and women's basketball and volleyball. It opened in 1954 and served as the basketball home court until 1998.

It was easy to go to work during basketball season; you just walked out the door and down the ramp to the floor.

G. Rollie White was torn down in 2013 to make room for the redevelopment of Kyle Field.

Two nicknames were used when talking about the building: "Jollie G. Rollie" and "The Holler House on the Brazos." There is no doubt in my mind that when filled to capacity at 7,800, it was the best home-court advantages in the SWC and the Big 12.

It was so loud that the announcers had to keep their headsets on and talk through the mic to communicate during time-outs. If the headsets were off, you had to get right next to that person's ear to be heard.

G. Rollie was originally meant to serve a dual purpose. The basketball floor could be removed to reveal a dirt floor. The dirt floor could then be used for an indoor rodeo. Billy Pickard told me that the floor was taken up one time, and they almost didn't get it back down. As far as he knew, they never tried that again.

Creatures lived in G. Rollie's hidden nooks and crannies. One year, a raccoon would come out from time to time and watch basketball practice from the stands. When I would work late, a creature would walk on the ceiling tiles, and I could see it move. I was always afraid a tile would give way and I would have unwanted company.

Many of the windows throughout the building would not close. Heating and air conditioning were a laughing matter. Our office was on the northwest corner, and when a cold front would pass through, the wind would move the curtains.

The open windows invited guests. It was not unusual to come back from lunch and find campus squirrels running across our desks. Sometimes they left in a hurry, and sometimes we left in a hurry if they seemed aggressive.

In my time at Texas A&M, I had offices at G. Rollie White Coliseum, the Koldus Building, Kyle Field, and Blue Bell Park.

I have a section of the wall of G. Rollie White, a piece of the original basketball floor, and one of the wooden bleachers as souvenirs. Future students at Texas A&M will have no idea what you mean when you say the "Holler House on the Brazos."

## The Aggies in the Air

During my 32 years of play-by-play, we flew everywhere! Most of the time we flew commercial, and then came charter flights, which helped student athletes miss less time away from class.

Football always flew a larger charter plane, as the team took 170-plus to each game. The broadcast crew was included, which made it easy on us.

That did not mean these trips didn't have their moments.

One such moment came on the flight back from St. Louis, Missouri, in 1998. The team had beaten Kansas State to win the Big 12 championship game. Every time any team won an away game, it was a happy flight back.

I was in the middle seat near the front of the plane. Leanne had the window seat, and Mike Ragan, a university police officer, was in the aisle seat. We started our descent to land.

Leanne, looking out the window, suddenly said she could see the McDonalds on highway 21 near the highway 6 bypass.

Mike looked and said the pilot was trying to land at Coulter Field in Bryan instead of Easterwood airport in College Station. The runway at Coulter Field is too short for a 737, which was the size of our plane. Without comment, the pilot gunned the engine and started back up in the air, apparently realizing the mistake. That would have been an interesting end of the day. Instead, we landed at Easterwood to a crowd of several thousand screaming Aggie fans.

One of the more recent flights was with the men's basketball team, flying back to College Station from San Juan, Puerto Rico. We had played the University of Dayton, the College of Charleston, and the New Mexico Lobos, going 2–1.

We were flying in a 737 with pilots and a crew that we all liked. The pilot came on the intercom and told us that there was a storm up ahead. He had requested that the plane be allowed to fly above or around it but was turned down.

I was watching a movie on my DVD player and stayed as focused as I could under the circumstances. If any passenger had been asleep, they were now awake and gripping the armrests. We hit a major air pocket, and our stomachs went up into our throats.

When we landed at Easterwood airport, Coach Kennedy's wife, Mary, asked our pilot how far we dropped in the air pocket. He said about 600 feet.

Baseball had a moment on a flight to Ames, Iowa. We flew two 18-seat prop planes on that trip. We had to land twice for fuel; first in Muskogee,

Oklahoma, and then in Topeka, Kansas. While we waited for fuel in Topeka, I wandered around the private terminal. I noticed the pilots in a room just off the main lobby. They were looking at a radar screen. Between Topeka and Ames was a big storm, and they were arguing about whether to fly around it or fly over it.

When they saw me listening in, I volunteered that flying around sounded like a good idea. Both agreed and said that's what would happen. *Not*!

We flew right over it, but the airplane wasn't powerful enough to fly above the weather, so we felt the storm. Most everyone on the two planes would agree later that it was the most intense 15 minutes of their lives.

When we landed, I found the two pilots and asked why we didn't fly around it. One of the pilots responded, "We fly cargo through that kind of weather all the time."

The baseball team was made up of human beings. Cargo? I don't think so!

Finally, men's basketball was flying back from Ames, and we drove to Des Moines to catch the charter. Good flight, no problems!

While we waited in the terminal, it was snowing outside, and visibility was limited. I noticed the music playing over the speakers, and it made me feel uneasy. It was a Buddy Holly song. Google Buddy Holly and Iowa for the rest of the story.

## Pigeons at the Games of Texas

Since the Summer Games of Texas began in 1986, Bryan–College Station has hosted the event seven times. This brought thousands of athletes, young and old, to the community to participate in everything from track and field to swimming, tennis, and golf—you name it.

A few years back, the closing ceremony for the event was held at Olsen Field (now Blue Bell Park at Olsen Field). I was asked to do the PA work for the ceremony, which was scripted. I had a walkie-talkie, as did a dozen or so other volunteers working down on the field and around the stadium.

I sat at a table in the third base dugout with a microphone and my walkie-talkie. There were risers placed in front of the pitcher's mound where the Children's Choir of Texas would stand to sing several patriotic songs.

Behind the risers and out of view of the crowd was a fellow with a large cage full of pigeons. On cue, he was to release them so they could fly over the choir and then over the stands. That was to be followed by the lights being turned off and fireworks over Olsen Field.

The cue was given to release the pigeons. At that point, the pigeon man put down his walkie-talkie, removed the sheet covering the cage, opened the door, and waited for the birds to fly out.

The sheet in this scenario was the key to what happened. With the sheet over the cage, the pigeons had all gone to roost, so not one pigeon came out. I could see the pigeon man from my vantage point in the dugout. He had his back turned to the risers and the stadium seating.

In a panic, he reached in and started throwing the sleeping birds back over his head, thinking they would fly. Instead, the stunned birds looked like they were doing cartwheels in the air before landing in front of the risers about halfway to home plate.

Meanwhile, someone was screaming on the walkie-talkie to stop throwing the pigeons. Pigeon man was nowhere near his walkie-talkie, so he kept sending a steady stream of "acrobatic pigeons" up over the risers.

Those poor birds were hitting the ground like wet sacks of cement and started walking around, stumbling and stunned. When almost all the birds had been catapulted out onto the field, someone killed the lights.

At the same moment, a local high school dance team started marching onto the field, where they would stand until the fireworks display was over and the lights were turned back on.

The young ladies had watched the cannon-balling pigeons and now found themselves walking through 40 or more birds. I distinctly heard one of them say, "I think I just stepped on one of those pigeons."

When the lights came back on, one of the "what just happened to me" birds sat right in front of me on my table. I started petting it on the head, and it made no effort to fly away. The crowd was laughing while the dance team tried to perform without injuring a bird.

When we were at last shutting it down, the last sight that I remember was the late Leo Goertz, the former head groundskeeper for all athletic fields at Texas A&M. Leo was standing with a water hose, wetting down the base path along the third base line with a pigeon riding shotgun on his left shoulder.

# 10

# Final Thoughts

## Albany, New York, January 24, 1995

This will be the second to last story. It starts with an incident that happened in Wichita Falls, Texas, when I was 10.

Back then, the city had a minor league baseball team called the Spudders (definition: a person who prepares and operates a rig for drilling oil wells). I was part of a group of boys whose fathers would take turns driving the group to a game at Spudder Park on the other side of town.

My father hosted the first trip because he was somewhat of a baseball fan. After we sat down in the stands, I noticed something that did not make sense to me. Down the right field line were some old rickety bleachers where the black fans sat.

I asked my dad why they couldn't sit with us. He said he would explain later, which he did, and for the first time in my life, I was introduced to racial prejudice. I made my mind up that evening never to be like that.

In January 1995, the Aggies traveled to Albany, New York, to play Siena College in our last nonconference game of the year. Our home engineer did not travel for this trip, so the network hired local talent to engineer the game.

The usual routine was for me to go to the team's practice session the night before the game to set up the radio equipment. This time, though, the Aggies had arrived too late and didn't go to the arena, so I called the local engineer and asked him to come pick up the equipment at our hotel.

He said he lived a long way from the hotel and asked if he could wait until tomorrow and pick up the equipment when we arrived at the arena. I explained that he needed to pick it up now because the team wouldn't get to the arena early enough for him to set up before the broadcast.

He knocked on my door an hour and a half later. He was about 5′4″ and weighed maybe 140 pounds. He had long hair that went below his belt in the back and looked like he had dressed in the dark. When I showed him the equipment, he said that it likely outweighed him, which it did. I loaded it in his car for him and said I would see him tomorrow night.

Walking back to the room, I wondered where the network found this guy and why his grooming and clothes were so shabby. Looking back, there was no doubt that I was rude to him.

I was holding my breath when the team arrived at the arena the next day, but to my great relief, he was there with his mother and his sister.

I still felt indignant toward him and answered with short, rude remarks. The mother tried to thank me for giving him the opportunity and the chance to make some extra money. I explained that I had nothing to do with that, as he had been hired by the network.

I sought out the Siena sports information director and asked if he had ever seen this fellow before. He said he had worked some games that year and apparently had done OK.

A few minutes before we were to go on the air, I finally asked if everything was working. He said that everything was OK and added that he was more nervous about this game than what was happening tomorrow.

"What's happening tomorrow?" I asked.

He replied, "I start my chemo for my cancer." His response hit me like a ton of bricks.

He might as well have been sitting on rickety bleachers in old Spudder Park. The attitude I swore I would never have had been present from the moment we met.

I couldn't have told you much about the game that night, but the Aggies did win, 76–70. I spent every time-out talking to my engineer, trying to make up for my awful behavior. We talked about where he went to school, his mother and sister, and who else had he engineered that year.

What I found was a nice young man with a big heart. When the game ended, I used what little time I had before the bus left to get his address and talk to his mom and sister.

When I got back to College Station, I sent him a gift box of Aggie gear and complimented him again on his work on the broadcast. I checked up on him every couple of months, and a little over a year later, he lost his battle with cancer. I learned a difficult lesson about judging someone, and I will never forget that young man and my poor behavior.

## My Testimony

In making plans to write this book, George Jacobus, the former college minister at our church, suggested that I use my testimony as the final chapter. George had heard it when he asked me to speak to a group of our college students. So here goes.

I accepted Christ as my personal savior in December 1960 at First Baptist Church, Wichita Falls. I am blessed to say that I was baptized by a great man of God, Dr. James H. Landes.

I was not raised in the church. My mother always encouraged me to go and would drop me off at the church nearest to our home until I had my own car.

I would like to say that I stayed strong in my faith, but I would drift away for a while and then come back. As an adult in Waco, I taught Sunday school, was a Sunday school superintendent, and even filled in for vacationing ministers at small churches in the Waco area. I worked at more Vacation Bible Schools than I could count. If the church doors were open, my family would be there.

That started to change as my career took off. The more my career threw at me, the more I threw away. I was 28, and people were patting me on the back, talking to me about sports, and wanting my opinion.

I was still going to church, but I was living a lie. God was no longer number one in my life. I could convince anyone that my walk was still strong, but my actions didn't back that up.

The marriage dissolved, and my focus turned solely to my work. It even overshadowed my desire to be a good father. I spent time with the boys, but it wasn't quality time.

My ego was out of control. I was rubbing elbows with big names in sports, politics, and show business. I remember being part of a program the day before a big bowl game, sitting at the head table with Miss America on my left and Joe Theismann on my right. So-called famous people knew me by my first name.

However, on the inside I was falling apart.

I had remarried, and my wife, Leanne, was a very godly woman. I was blessed to have her. She stayed with me despite my reluctance to go to church, my language, my temper, and my drinking.

Texas A&M hired me for two reasons—my ability to broadcast football, basketball, and baseball games and my sales experience. Those two talents gave me the best of two worlds. I loved doing the games, and I loved selling what we had to offer our clients in sports sponsorships.

My life was spiraling downward when one January day, I made a sales call to Austin to visit Dirk Dozier, who was then the president of Austaco. This company owned numerous Taco Bells in Central Texas, including Bryan–College Station.

Dirk had a strong walk with Christ and openly shared his faith. We had many talks in his office about how God was working in his life. I was too ashamed to share how I was slipping into a deep pit and saw no way out.

On that visit, Dirk talked about a book that he had read and encouraged me to read it as soon as possible. I pulled out a three-by-five card, jotted down the title, and said I would buy it. Those were hollow words. When I got home that night, I put the card in a stack of cards on my desk and forgot it.

May rolled around, and my life was not any better. I was not sleeping at night and my anxiety attacks were long and hard to stop. Leanne had gone to Midland for our niece's graduation. I had a baseball series at Olsen Field. When I got home that night, I grabbed some beers, sat down on the couch, and turned on the television. I passed out on the couch and never made it to bed. When I woke up the next morning, I had a terrific headache.

Let me stop right here for a minute.

Have you seen the movie *War Room*? If you did, you may remember the scene where the husband breaks down and cries because he realizes that he had forgotten his wife and daughter to chase his profession. With God's help, he repents, recovers, and works to save his marriage. When I saw that scene in the theater, I started crying hard.

Back to my testimony.

I got up from the couch, went to my office, sat down, and put my head on the desk. The next thing I know, I am on the floor with my face buried in the carpet, crying like a baby. Crying as hard as I ever cried in my life. I finally pulled myself back up to the chair and had some terrible thoughts go through my mind—really bad thoughts.

Then, out loud I said, "Father, I want Jesus back in my life. I can't go on like this!" Remember the Dirk Dozier suggestion? His card was at the top of the stack of business cards on my desk.

I grabbed the card, got dressed, and drove to the bookstore to buy that book. When I walked in, it was on display right by the front door.

The first page said it was a 40-day read, one chapter a day, and you needed a partner. I called Leanne in Midland and told her that I had bought a book and it said I needed to read it with a partner.

She asked what it was, and I told her. She said our sister-in-law had given her a copy the night before, and she agreed to read it with me. When she got home, she related two instances—one in the airport and one on the plane—where people saw the book and told her it would change her life.

We started the book that Monday. Forty chapters in 40 days. The book's opening sentence hit us both right between the eyes: "It's not about you." The book, of course, is Rick Warren's *Purpose Driven Life*.

Everything that I wanted to leave my life left that Monday: the anxiety attacks, the temper fits, getting drunk, the foul language, and the poor behavior.

Now some 15 years later, God has brought me along as he wants and not as I might want. He has given me many opportunities to share my testimony, has led me back to reading the Bible, and has given me a mission or two.

I have said this to many people in these last few years: "Never let what you do be who you are." I am first a child of God, second a husband, third a father and grandfather, and lastly, a broadcaster.

I walked away from Him at 28 and came back at 59, so it's never too late. I will never be without Him again, and I know I have the promise of eternity because of His Son, Jesus Christ.

Never let what you do be who you are.

My life verse is Hebrews 12:1 and 2a: "Therefore, since we also have such a large cloud of witnesses surrounding us, let us lay aside every hindrance and the sin that so easily ensnares us. Let us run with endurance the race that lies before us, keeping our eyes on Jesus, the source and perfecter of our faith."

## Deciding to Retire

In August 2017, I released the following statement concerning my retirement:

> "God assigns certain jobs for certain times. While it's important to respond obediently, it's also vital we understand when an assignment is finished. Diligence and job completion honor the Lord, but resistance to change and refusal to let go can hinder His plan" (from *Journey*, June 15, 2017, page 23; Lifeway Press, Nashville, TN).

The 2017–2018 season will mark my 48th year in collegiate broadcasting, and next month I will celebrate my 72nd birthday. In discussions that started a year ago this August with Texas A&M Ventures, as well as with my wife, Leanne, we have decided that the 2017 Texas A&M football season and the 2017–2018 men's basketball season will be my last with both teams. I will continue doing play-by-play for the Aggie baseball team on a year-by-year basis.

There will be many people to thank as we make our way through this coming year. I will start with coach Jackie Sherrill and the late Ralph Carpenter, who extended the offer to be the voice of the Aggies prior to the 1985 season. My association with Texas A&M University and its athletic department has truly been a blessing. The friendships and the joy of broadcasting all these games are beyond words.

I'm also honored to have worked with every entity that has held the broadcast rights to Texas A&M athletics. For those of you who have been around for a long time, you will understand this statement: I am the last of the Southwest Conference Exxon Network announcers still active in sports broadcasting!

To the Aggies and radio listeners who have been so gracious and kind for these many years, thank you for your words, texts, emails, Facebook messages, and letters. I am humbled by your thoughtful generosity.

Knowing God has a plan for every day of our lives, I look forward to the future and what He has in store for Leanne and me!

This statement went out in early August 2017, and I have had no second thoughts about retiring. In the summer of 2018, Texas A&M announced that Andrew Monaco from San Antonio would move into the radio booth beginning in August 2018. I wish him well and much success. I know the Aggie family will embrace him as they did me.

Since my announcement, I had two emotional moments that brought tears to my eyes. The first came in Houston. Dave Elmendorf introduced me when I was presented with the Ron Stone Award by the Houston Touchdown Club. He had asked the Los Angeles Dodgers if they could get Vin Scully to salute my retirement on video, which he graciously did. Vin Scully is one of my broadcast heroes. As I told Dave that night, that video blew me away.

The second time happened in 2018 right before a home basketball game. A gentleman came up and asked if we were on the air, and I said no. He started to speak and then started crying. He apologized and asked for a few seconds to regain his composure. When he did, he said, "I don't know what I am going to do without you on the radio," and then walked away.

I started crying and had to sit down. My regret is that I did not get his name. That sentiment came from that man's heart, and I would like to tell him thank you.

## The 2018 National Football Foundation Chris Schenkel Award and My Thoughts

The official release announcing this great honor read as follows:

### Irving, Texas (May 30, 2018)

The National Football Foundation (NFF) and College Hall of Fame announced that Texas A&M University broadcaster Dave South, who called his last Aggie football season in 2017, will be the recipient of the 2018 NFF Chris Schenkel Award. He will officially be honored December 4 during the 61st NFF Annual Awards Dinner at the New York Hilton Midtown.

Presented annually since 1996, the award recognizes individuals who have had long, distinguished careers broadcasting college football with direct ties to a specific university. The award is named in honor of its inaugural recipient Chris Schenkel, the longtime ABC Sports broadcaster who emceed the NFF Annual Awards dinner for 28 consecutive years from 1968 to 1995.

South almost completely retired from broadcasting in 1984, but Texas A&M head coach and athletics director Jackie Sherrill asked South to fill in for one season at Kyle Field in 1985, which led to his more than three decades calling Aggie football, basketball, and baseball games.

South has been on the call for some the Texas A&M's more memorable game, including the 1986 Cotton Bowl, when A&M beat Auburn and College Football Hall of Famer Bo Jackson; Hall of Fame coach R. C. Slocum's win over No. 1 Oklahoma in 2002; and the Johnny Manziel-led victory at No. 1 Alabama in 2012.

His call of running back Sirr Parker's winning touchdown in the 1998 Big 12 championship game against Kansas State was selected as on the top 100 calls of the 20th century and was featured in a book and CD.

South also served as A&M's associate athletics director for sponsorships and broadcasting through 2009, prior to focusing on his broadcasting duties in semiretirement.

Here is a list of the previous Chris Schenkel Award recipients:

1996: Chris Schenkel (ABC Sports)
1997: Jack Cristil (Mississippi State)
1998: Max Falkenstein (Kansas)
1999: Jack Fleming (West Virginia)
2000: Ray Christensen (Minnesota)
2001: Frank Fallon (Baylor)
2002: Bob Brooks (Iowa)
2003: Larry Munson (Georgia)
2004: Bob Robertson (Washington State)
2005: Tony Roberts (Notre Dame)

2006: Johnny Holiday (Maryland)

2007: Bill Hillgrove (Pittsburgh)

2008: Bob Curtis (Idaho) and Dick Galiette (Yale)

2009: Larry Zimmer (Colorado)

2010: Joe Starkey (California)

2011: Woody Durham (North Carolina)

2012: Bob Barry Sr. (Oklahoma)

2013: Gene Deckerhoff (Florida State)

2014: Frank Beckmann (Michigan)

2015: Jim Hawthorne (LSU)

2016: Bob Rondeau (Washington)

2017: Jon Teicher (University of Texas at El Paso)

2018: Dave South (Texas A&M)

Naturally I recognize many of the names on this list and feel deeply honored to be included. These men obviously made an impact on college football through their work as broadcasters. Following are some thoughts on some of the honorees.

Frank Fallon, the 2001 honoree, was my mentor for many years, and I learned a great deal in working with him. Frank was a professional in every sense of the word. He could have worked at the highest level of this profession but chose instead to stay at Baylor, his first love.

Bob Barry Sr., the 2012 honoree, was loved by Sooner fans everywhere. He was a true gentleman and made everyone who met him feel like a friend.

Jim Hawthorne, the 2015 honoree, and I met long before Texas A&M joined the SEC. He and I visited during his last season calling LSU football and basketball.

Our thoughts mirrored one another on retirement. Neither of us had any regrets about our decision and were looking forward to the future.

I have heard many stories about other recipients, and in each case, you would hear that they were professionals who loved what they did.

# The Cycle of Life

I find it amusing how life runs in circles, or cycles, as we get older. At the time of this writing, I am 73 years old, and a couple of things have surfaced, or rather, resurfaced.

The first is a weekly music show on KAMU FM, Bryan–College Station's PBS station. I got the idea from Jim Hawthorne, the long-time broadcaster at LSU, who retired in 2017 after 35 years as the play-by-play announcer.

On his last trip to College Station for basketball, he and I visited to discuss his retirement plans. He and his wife had to put off traveling because of his schedule, so first they planned to travel.

He also told me that early in his career, he had been a disc jockey (DJ) and had talked the program director at a Baton Rouge radio station into giving him a couple hours once a week to do a '60s-flavored country music show.

What a great idea! I had been a disc jockey back in the day, playing rock and roll music of the late '50s through the mid-1960s.

Jim's idea was such a good one, I decided to try it.

I approached staff at KAMU FM, our PBS station, about a one-hour radio show featuring music from the 1950s and mid-'60s, and they said yes. For that I want to say thank you.

The show first aired on Saturday, October 6, 2018, at 5 p.m. It repeats on Sunday at noon and is prerecorded in my home studio.

It's been more fun than I imagined. Today you can download songs and research material on music and entertainers that simply was not available in the early '60s.

By some standards, perhaps this isn't a lot, but I easily have some 17,000 titles, and I have found a long list of songs that I played during my DJ career.

When I announced that I would start the radio show, I was surprised at friends who said that they too had been DJs.

I've also come full circle with my trike. When I was five or six, I had a tricycle that I rode in my grandparent's neighborhood at breakneck speed. Now almost 70 years later, I have a motorcycle with three wheels, but I wouldn't dare ride it at breakneck speed!

There is life after retirement, so own it and live it!

Now let's go for a ride and get back to the music.

# Index